ENGLISH INSTITUTIONS

GENERAL EDITOR

SIR GEORGE BARNES

ENGLISH
RELIGIOUS DISSENT

BY

ERIK ROUTLEY

B.D., M.A., D.Phil.

*Sometime Mackennal Lecturer and Tutor in
Ecclesiastical History, Mansfield College, Oxford. Minister of
Augustine-Bristo Congregational Church, Edinburgh*

CAMBRIDGE

AT THE UNIVERSITY PRESS

1960

PUBLISHED BY
THE SYNDICS OF THE CAMBRIDGE UNIVERSITY PRESS

Bentley House, 200 Euston Road, London, N.W. 1
American Branch: 32 East 57th Street, New York 22, N.Y.

©

CAMBRIDGE UNIVERSITY PRESS
1960

Printed in Great Britain at the University Press, Cambridge
(Brooke Crutchley, University Printer)

AUTHOR'S PREFACE

Now that it is written, but before any reader reads it, I am sure that certain apologies and warnings are due in respect of the following pages. I have been asked to write about English religious Dissent as an English institution. I gather, then, that my readers are expected to be among those intelligent persons who are interested in many things about which they know little. I do not gather that they will be primarily learned Dissenters themselves. I write here for the man who has the sense to be interested in Dissent as an English institution just as he might be interested in Parliament, or railways, or the police, or cricket as English institutions—part of the familiar scenery which he has always been aware of, but about which it occurs to him that it would be good to know more.

Therefore I am sure it is not my business to defend Dissent. I shall here possibly offend Dissenters by not always insisting on the rightness of the Dissenting side of an argument. Nor, as one of them, am I concerned to paint them blacker than Chesterton and Belloc painted them—although another English institution, that of 'sportsmanship', widely practised by those who

> praise with enthusiastic tone
> All centuries but this and every country but their own

in religious contexts might have led me to do so.

Nor—and here I shall really be in trouble—have I scrupled to omit things which I am sure will not interest my intelligent inquirer. My judgement may well have been at fault, and he may be greatly bored by what I have thought it right to put in. But I think that he wants to know what Dissent now is, what it began by being, what is the broad outline of its story, and what justification we have for calling it an English institution. That I have done my best to tell him. I do not think he wants from me long lists of venerable Dissenting names—ministers, missionaries, Lord Mayors of London and eminent shopkeepers; and if he did expect me to dwell lovingly on the men of public fame who have been Dissenters, I happen to believe that to do so would have been sharp practice, and no service to his understanding of the essence of Dissent. He will, of course, find all he wants, should he think of pursuing the subject, in the books to which reference is made in the notes.

I must also say that I have not thought it necessary to say anything at all about Dissent in Wales or in Scotland. In both those countries the story is quite different from the English story. They demand separate books to themselves. Dissent in Scotland, for example, is represented by Congregationalism, the Baptists, the Methodists, and the Episcopal Church: Presbyterianism in Scotland is not Dissent. That makes a world of difference. And the story in Wales is even more complicated and interesting. But I felt that this was excluded by the word 'English' in the title given me, and in any case the book would have had to be three times its present length if justice were done to those cultures.

But the editor of this series has seen fit to regard Dissent as an English institution. That, as I cannot help repeating in the text of what follows, is the greatest thing of all. The reader will soon see how much Dissenters in their heroic days owed to the hospitality of the University of Cambridge. To their 'conspiracy of praise' one more obscure voice now joins itself.

E.R.

EDINBURGH
1959

CONTENTS

PLATES

CHAPTER I

INTRODUCTION

1. '*Alternative Government*'

In the year 1937, in the reign of King George VI, the Leader of 'His Majesty's Opposition' in the House of Commons was for the first time granted an official salary. Of this one commentator wrote, 'That must be a strange sight for the foreign observer: every British Government paying its principal critic handsomely for his criticism'.[1] The truth is that the awarding of this payment marked the recognition by the British public, through its Government, that the principle of a permanent Opposition was, and had long been, an English institution in politics. It was, after all, little more than the writing down for the first time of one of the most precious unwritten paragraphs in the British constitution. The principle had established itself long before. Near the beginning of the nineteenth century John Cam Hobhouse, M.P. (later Lord Broughton of Gyfford), coined the phrase 'His Majesty's Opposition' half in jest; and the context of that coinage makes it obvious that he, in a less official manner, was recognizing an already well-established principle. At some stage in its political evolution the British people came to be convinced that good government would be better ensured on the part of any party in power if it could count on an Opposition which constantly and as of duty offered an alternative government.

It was about the time when the Opposition was thus written firmly into the constitution that Dr Nathaniel Micklem wrote two highly significant sentences on the subject of English Dissent. 'If Nonconformity does not offer an alternative government to the Church of England', he said, 'it cannot appeal to the allegiance of the nation; it confesses itself sectarian. I believe that it should offer an "alternative government" to the Church of England, and that, if it will not do so, it is, in fact, disloyal to its own principles.'[2] It is no accident, even though it might seem at first to be a paradox, that those words were written by one of Nonconformity's most eminent ecumenical statesmen: by the joint-chairman of the Lambeth Conversations of 1948–50. But neither is it an accident that it was written by a churchman who, himself the son of an M.P., has always involved himself in political affairs and has been President of the Liberal Party.

Dr Micklem was, in those two sentences, bringing into focus a general, but up to then unexpressed, opinion that English Dissent is in some sense to be thought of as an English institution. The manner of his statement carries also a strong suggestion that Dissent is to an important extent a political matter. In this he is unquestionably right. To say that Dissent is political is to say both more and less than that Dissent leans towards this or that party in modern politics, or even in the politics of the days of its foundation. The close association of Dissent with the Liberal Party at the turn of the present century is almost an historical accident compared with the vital importance of another sense in which it is political. What matters much more is this: that when we are discussing Dissent we are treating of the Church in its most human, not to say fallible, aspect. Politics is the behaviour of men who must live with one another in a society; and the history of Dissent is the story of how Christians in England have lived with one another, and of what various success they

2

achieved in that aim. But as the story unfolds itself we are
able to see another larger story behind and beyond it—the
story of the development of doctrine. Church history
seems to suggest that the building up of doctrine, and the
implanting of good doctrine in the mind and affections of
one generation after another, seems to require a principle
of Dissent in order that it may be achieved. This is not the
place to argue the theology of that assertion: it is in itself
probably a comment on the fallibility of human nature, and
it would be unwise to insist that the violence, bigotry and
gracelessness of church controversy was in the design that
Christ had for his church. Much of church history, indeed,
comments bitterly on the text 'It must needs be that
offences will come: but woe unto him by whom the offence
cometh'.

It is clear, indeed, that if we allow theological passion to
invade these pages we shall stultify the object that their
publisher has in mind. We must take care not to be too sure
that all Dissent was always wrong, or that it was always
right. That is why I introduce at the very outset that comment of Dr Micklem's. For there is a sense in which
Dissent has now become an English institution: but it is
important to recognize what a remarkable thing it is that it
should be possible to write as objectively about it as I hope
to succeed in writing.

Dissent has been until recently—and in some quarters
is still held to be—a defensive and strident minority of
religious sectaries. Even though it be true that 'The British
cherish their minorities',[3] this is a minority which the
British have found it very hard to cherish. To the mind of
the ordinary Englishman it has presented itself now as
grim and formidable, now as contemptible. The Dissenting
chapel erected opposite the vicarage gate in Trollope's

3

The Vicar of Bullhampton is a symbol of what most ordinary Anglicans took to be the attitude of Nonconformity in the mid-nineteenth century. The lampoons on back-street Bethels which fashionably adorned the novels of the 'thirties are another aspect of the same view, or attributed view. In present-day English fiction, where the Anglican parson is getting a much better press than he had before the Second World War, the Dissenter scarcely appears. He is still, if not now a tiresome and despicable figure, an unromantic one. Nonconformity has rarely, if ever, commanded the affection, even if now and again it has commanded the fear and respect, of the Englishman. At times it has behaved vilely and brought on itself troubles about which it has complained loudly, but which can hardly be regarded otherwise than as induced by Dissent's own obstinate and high-principled tactlessness.

But it is as well to admit what there can be no real doubt about, namely, that Dissent in the broadest sense, Dissent not only religious but secular as well, is as English an institution as the House of Commons itself. Perhaps it is because religious Dissent moves in the one sphere where the issues are larger than those handled by Parliament, that it provides more precipitous paradoxes, more lurid atrocity stories, wilder inconsistencies, than does the story of Parliament. But it is entirely necessary, in order to understand English religious Dissent, to keep in view the fact that it is undoubtedly and irretrievably English.

Moreover, I believe it to be right thus to usher in its story with a political analogy, because just as the members of the English nation and the members of the English churches share a common humanity, the factors which make the British constitution what it is have likewise operated, in another field, to make the pattern of British

4

(or at any rate English) church life what it is. It will undoubtedly strike ecumenically-minded readers as intoler-
ably complacent to say so: but if by any chance those who
regard a movement towards religious uniformity in world
Protestantism as a desirable thing dare to overlook the
difference between the English form of Dissent and those
Dissents which prevail in other cultures, they will see no
fruit of their labours better than paper.

The story of the development of English Dissent is not,
strictly, the story of something that has been in existence
for four hundred years. It is better regarded as the story of
the emergence from very remote beginnings of something
that has quite recently taken on itself the form familiar to
contemporary Englishmen. In the introductory chapter
of his *The Jacobite Movement* Sir Charles Petrie wrote:

To understand the attitude both of Charles and of his opponents
it must be realized that no one had yet conceived as possible the
existence of more than one Church. To-day, if a man finds the
Anglican service too High or too Low for his taste he is at perfect
liberty to attend a Nonconformist or Roman Catholic place of
worship, but in the seventeenth century he had no such choice.
The aim of everyone was to make the Church of England what
he thought a Church should be.[4]

The notion of a tolerated and even respected Dissent is
entirely foreign to all ages of English church history before
1900. The notion of Dissent as an English institution,
rather than as an English embarrassment, has no place in
English thought before that date. How we came by what
we have now, it will be the business of this book to explain.
But it must be understood at once that part of the story
will remain hidden, even as part of the story of the British
constitution remains hidden. It is very much a matter of
changes of opinion and social habit, of relaxation of what
at one time appeared essential disciplines, of new and not

always responsible evaluations of principle, which cannot be ascribed to this person or that movement, and can be recognized only by the symptoms they produced in the life of the nation and the Church.

It is hardly yet true to say that Dissent means to most Anglicans what Opposition means to most members of the governing party. And of course there is one vital sense in which the analogy between Dissent and Opposition does not meet the case. For while Opposition offers always an alternative government, Dissent stands not for alternative government (for all Christians agree that the Head of the Church is Christ), but for alternative *forms* of government. Dissent has never stood positively as a whole for a re-writing of the classic Creeds, even though it has sometimes stood for an unorthodox attitude towards them; it has very rarely stood for the abolition of the two biblical sacraments, even though certain parties in Dissent did and do declare them unnecessary to salvation. In those senses Dissent is not 'alternative government'. But in its continuous criticism of certain habits of thought about the regulation of the visible church, in its constant questioning of certain assertions which in other quarters are regarded as axioms, Dissent forms something like a permanent Opposition.

It must be admitted that Dissenters are men who live dangerously. The spiritual perils of Dissent are obvious to Dissenters only in times when Dissent is not obliged to be violent. Dissent can be truculent, temperamental and proud. When it is active it is rarely gifted with a sense of humour or proportion. It is very rarely indeed the product of pure motives. Anybody, after all, can dissent from what proves inconvenient to him or inimical to the way of life that he has, on insufficient consideration of his obligations

6

to society, chosen. Anybody can dissent, and gain much credit for dissenting, from what he has never troubled to understand. The late Mgr Ronald Knox, in his book, *Caliban in Grub Street*, mercilessly exposed the follies of eminent journalists and authors who were widely applauded for dissenting from doctrines which they attributed to Christians but which Christians did not hold; and the generation which brought forth that book and the futilities that gave rise to it was one in which very large credit was to be had for dissenting from what had never been understood or patiently evaluated. Corruptions of that kind are to be found in the history of orthodox Dissent, and they are still there among many who would be scornful of the flounderings of the neo-Georgian aesthetic agnostics.

That is why the history of Dissent brings into the foreground so high a proportion of characters who are admirable without being attractive, pious without being especially pleasant. Dissent, for most of its life, has been a minority, and began as a minority under severe censure and even persecution. It is not to be wondered at if Dissent not infrequently showed the symptoms of mild paranoia. What matters is that Dissent at present is something which is enough of an English institution to provide a subject for such a book as this one.

2. *On the use of the word 'Dissent'*

It will be clear from what I have so far written that I want the word 'Dissent' understood in its primary sense of 'responsible minority opinion'. But that is not the sense which 'Dissent' normally carries in the church histories, and for the reader's convenience I must distinguish certain other senses in which the word is used.

'Dissenters', as a name for a religious denomination, is a word of limited applications. It was first applied in the course of the Westminster Assembly (1644–6) to the seven 'dissenting brethren' who took issue with the majority of the Presbyterian divines in that conclave on the matter of church government. What they said will be more fully recounted in chapter VI. It is sufficient here to say that if we take the true historical meaning of 'Dissenter' it means simply 'Congregationalist'.

When we come to the eighteenth century 'Dissent' clearly carries a wider meaning. The 'Dissenting Deputies', of whom again we shall have to say more in their place (chapter VIII), were chosen from Presbyterian, Baptist and Congregationalist churches, and in 1732, at the foundation of that body, 'Dissent' meant the whole body of those who were not communicant members of and habitual worshippers with the Church of England. In fact, it meant by then 'Nonconformity'.

It is doubtful whether there is any clear historical justification for including the Methodist connection within the word 'Dissent'. Up to the year 1784 the Methodists were never by intention in schism from the Church of England. John Wesley's 'ordinations' are the only argument for saying that they separated themselves. But after that date, when the Methodist Conference was inaugurated, Methodism was a separate denomination, and in our own time we are accustomed to the fact that Methodism is out of communion with the Church of England, and is a powerful member of the Free Church Federal Council. That is sufficient ground for assuming that nowadays 'Dissent' means 'non-Anglicanism' or 'Free Churchmanship', even if 'Dissent' is not a word which Methodists care to apply to themselves.

Despite these ambiguities, it seems good to keep the word 'Dissent' as a primary term of reference: 'Nonconformity', though it is originally a strong and colourful word, has too many Victorian associations to be an adequate word for what we are really discussing here. 'Free Churchmanship' is altogether too modern a term to apply to classic Puritanism. Anything else is too negative to be useful. I am anxious to keep before the reader the principle of Dissent, a principle of wider than merely ecclesiastical import, and this is the only word that has not an exclusively religious, not to say denominational sense. It is, therefore, the word we shall chiefly be using.

CHAPTER II

BACKGROUND, A.D. 200–1562

1. *The English Reformation was not merely political*

In a famous opening sentence, Sir Maurice Powicke declared roundly that 'the one definite thing which can be said about the Reformation in England is that it was an act of state'.[1] To read over the primary documents of the English Reformation as they are collected, for example, in Gee and Hardy's compendium,[2] and then to read over the corresponding documents of the continental Reformation in Kidd's collection,[3] is to be reminded at once of the truth of this statement. The authors of Reformation in England, where 'Reformation' means the movement towards an English Establishment under the supreme governorship of the English Crown, were first and last King Henry VIII and Queen Elizabeth I, and the primary documents are largely issued in their names. The primary documents of the continental Reformation are written by the theologians. The English Reformation, furthermore, was accompanied by a great deal more religious bloodshed than was that on the Continent. There is nothing in the history of the continental Reformation from 1517 to the death of Calvin (1564) to correspond with the line of martyrs, both Catholic and Protestant, which the English Reformation produced within the same period.

The whole texture of the English Reformation was determined by the fact that its efficient cause was a controversy at the highest possible political level. Contrasting the condition of England in the fifteen-thirties with that of the Continent, T. A. Lacey put it thus: 'What happened was that at the very height of the Continental movement, England was in the grasp of a stubbornly Catholic King, who had a personal quarrel with the Pope.'[4] The leader of the German Reformation did not have the country in his grasp, was very far from being a stubborn Catholic, and had no personal quarrel with the Pope, to whom his private life was of no consequence at all.

Anybody hearing for the first time about the English Reformation, and introduced to it along these lines, might reasonably say, 'Then I may take it that the whole affair was political from beginning to end?' But that is where he would have to be corrected. It is impossible to reform a church by political means. Theologians prefer to say that it is impossible for it to be reformed otherwise than by the Word of God. But when the political controversy is between the head of a State and the head of the universal visible Church, the Church in the State governed by the rebellious monarch is bound, unless it rebels itself against its king, to suffer some kind of reformation.

The church is not, in the secular sense, a primarily political body. If, therefore, you attempt to reform its government, having in mind nothing beyond the political expediency of substituting this constitution for that, this theory of government for that, and having in mind no doctrinal issue whatever, you will none the less, with your first reconstructive move, release theological issues with which you had not reckoned; and in the end you will have to accept those pressures as normative of the pattern that your new church government will take. To put it thus parabolically is to insist that this is a general principle, not merely a description of what happened to Henry VIII and Elizabeth I. Henry VIII was, as everybody knows, doctrinally innocent. Pope Leo X had given him the title

'Defender of the Faith' in recognition of the orthodoxy of his pamphlet *Assertio Septem Sacramentorum* which he wrote against Luther in 1521. Except in as much as some may believe his defiance of the Pope and his personal sexual aberrations to be inseparable from false doctrine, there could hardly be a clearer case of purely political reform than that which he urged on the English Church. There certainly was no clearer case in all the sections of the European Reformation. And yet, considered as a purely political reform, the enterprise was doomed to failure. For none but a theological innocent could really conceive that to substitute the supreme headship of the English monarch in the Church for the supreme headship of the Pope was a purely political act. It could not possibly be a mere reorientation of authorities, for the very simple reason that there was already in England—and there would have been in any country—a body of opinion which, whatever it thought about the Pope's supreme headship, cared a good deal less for the supreme headship of the King. From its very inception, therefore, the English Reformation was shot through with a theological colour given to it by the presence of a public opinion that looked for Reformation on principle, Reformation of a religious kind, and cared nothing for any political Reformation that did not satisfy their religious assumptions. This body of opinion, which had been there since Wyclif (and which I propose to argue had been there long even before him), held in check to some extent by the prevailing structure of Catholicism while it extended to England, was abruptly released when that structure showed signs of finally collapsing. Henry VIII never lived to see the full fruit of this uprising of popular opinion after 1558; but he could have foreseen it had he been less preoccupied with his 'personal quarrel with the Pope'.

2. *The Englishness of the English Dissenting principle*

There is, then, a large difference in polarity between what the courtiers and some of the bishops took for 'Reformation' in England, and what a considerable body of popular opinion took for 'Reformation'. Since it is from this body of opinion that English Dissent springs directly, we must here look back into history and see whence it came.

Christianity was brought very early to Britain, partly by Christian members of the Roman army and Christian merchants who engaged in trade with these islands, partly, no doubt, by missionaries. Tertullian, writing about A.D. 200, pays special attention to the spread of Christianity in this direction. Arguing for the Faith on the grounds of what it has achieved, he wrote,

In whom else have all the nations believed, than in the Christ who has already come? Parthians and other nations, such as different races of the Gaetuli, many borders of the Mauri, all the confines of Spain and various tribes of Gaul; also places in Britain which, though inaccessible to the Romans, have yielded to Christ; and districts among the Sarmatae, the Dacians, the Germans, the Scythians and many remote peoples, provinces and islands unknown to us which we are unable to reckon.[5]

It may be too much to argue, as Hugh Williams did,[6] that Tertullian's special reference to Britain is more than a rhetorical flourish which might as well cover the whole list of places he enumerates. But what is interesting in Tertullian's sentence is the fact that by A.D. 200 Christianity was flourishing to some extent in these islands, and that, according to him, its dissemination here was not primarily due to the efficiency of the Roman armed conquest.

It is further on record that during the third century these islands, though technically part of the Roman Empire, were virtually separated from it during two periods (about

259–72 and 286–96) when the Roman administration was
too hard-pressed to maintain its garrison here. It is
generally thought that the only widespread Roman persecution of Christians which had any effect in Britain was
that either of Decius (249–51) or of Valerian (258–9),during
one of which it is supposed that the group of martyrs
gathered round St Alban perished. It is certainly probable
that the equally violent and general persecution usually
attributed to Diocletian (A.D. 303–4) had no effect here
at all.[7]

A little later, in the fifth century, came the two celebrated
collisions between the Celtic Church and Catholic orthodoxy—the controversy between Pelagius and Augustine
of Hippo which continued through the years 405–15, and
the excommunication of the British Church by Pope Leo I
in 454 on the ground of its refusal to come into line with
Catholic practice on the date of the celebration of Easter.
Along with this divergence, certain other customs which
disagreed with Roman practice were brought to the Pope's
notice, customs tending on the whole away from clericalism and close diocesan organization of the metropolitan kind, and although too much must not be gathered
from these matters, it is quite safe to conclude that the
Celtic Church, no doubt by reason of its physical isolation,
exhibited a tendency to be out of step with, and when
pressed to insist on nonconformity to, the customs that
prevailed at the centre of Catholicism.

With the advent of Augustine, first archbishop of
Canterbury (597), whose work it was to preach Christianity
not to the Celtic Christians but to those heathen Teutonic
invaders who had driven them into Wales and the West
Country, the picture altered importantly. At the synods
of Whitby, Hatfield and Hertford, matters controversial

14

between the British and the newly converted English Christians were to some extent clarified, and the English Church settled down to a pattern based on contemporary continental models. But a large section of the British, or Celtic, population was never convinced by the Augustinian reforms, and, turning their backs on them and looking towards Ireland and Scotland, part of the Celtic Church formed itself into a settled Dissent against the Roman–Catholic–English system instituted by Augustine's followers.

It is one of the ironies of history that this Dissent of Celt against Teuton has in our own time survived in two forms of Dissent against the English Establishment very widely separated from each other. On the one hand, we have Irish Catholicism, which is defiantly critical of all English Protestant values, and is not infrequently an embarrassment to English Catholicism: on the other there is the native culture of Wales which, since the Calvinist Revival of the eighteenth century has given itself equally firmly to the forms of Protestant Dissent. Both cultures are critical of 'English' culture, both lead to fierce nationalisms. They disagree radically in the forms taken by their respective Dissents, but at bottom the fact of the Dissent can be traced all the way back to the curious and unexampled situation that prevailed when Augustine of Canterbury first set foot in Britain. Augustine and his followers were faced with an already suspicious and Dissenting Celtic Church which looked with modified enthusiasm on the Roman evangelization of their Teutonic enemies, and with positive horror on a church organization that would bring a combined authority of metropolitan Rome and baptized Teuton to bear on the Celts, who had worshipped Christ in their own way for five centuries.

English Christianity cannot now be called primarily Celtic. The right way to read this strange chapter of history is to see in the Celtic Dissent a principle of insular conservatism, a principle of 'primitiveness', which has manifested itself in many other ways since, but which is to be seen at regular intervals throughout the English story. There is always a tendency in these islands to say to Rome, 'Our way of worship, and our conception of authority, is authentic and primitive. We learned it from the same sources that taught it to you. But we do not necessarily accept the developments on it that you have accepted. We go to the source, from which here and there you have strayed.'

In a way it was easier to say that in A.D. 650 than it was in 1559; and it was easier to say it in 1559 than it is in the small world of 1959. And yet all the things that happened to the inhabitants of these islands during the Middle Ages to form them into the British nation did not lessen this curious centrifugal tendency in the nation's faith. Rather it strengthened it. Britain suffered its last violent invasion from the Continent in 1066. Yet nowhere is there such a mixture of races and cultures as there is in England, except in modern America. Ancient English families, proud of their lineage, bear names that originated in France, in Germany, in Holland, in Scandinavia and, of course, in Jewry; it is beyond Offa's Dyke and the Tweed that the Celtic names predominate. England, in the Middle Ages, grew into a very special kind of 'city', and became a focus of European civilization, yet physically separate from Europe. Its hospitality was to a unique degree the hospitality of the open door and of the closed door: the hospitality that welcomes the guest and the hospitality that keeps him as a resident. England became the most intractable member of the Holy Roman Empire—never really a member of it at all. It was, in the days of Bede and Alcuin, Aldhelm and John the Scot, a source of curious and devoted culture. Charles the Great depended primarily on Alcuin of Northumbria for his education. It was intractable not so much because of the open defiance of its kings—the medieval Popes suffered much more violent affront from the continentals than they did from the English. It was intractable rather in what must have appeared to the Papacy its maddening self-sufficiency, its quiet neglect of certain externals of Catholic allegiance, which was only now and again stirred into open rebellion by some special incident. England was, in the Middle Ages, asking radical questions about the 'City' which continental Catholicism was not really equipped to answer.

So that, while no European state has a clean record so far as disputes with the Papacy are concerned, there is discernible an obstinate tendency in England to defy certain axioms of catholicity. The important part of this is not so much King John's breach with the Pope, or Bishop Grosseteste's spectacular action in sending packing from a Lincoln prebend some obscure relative whom the Pope had intruded into it, nor even the events that led to the Statutes of *Provisors* and *Praemunire*; it is rather what the author of *Piers Plowman* puts his finger on when he makes a typical English squire, talking religion over his table after a day's hunting, deny the doctrine of original sin.

> Why for the works of Adam should we who are living
> Rot and be rent? Reason denies it.[8]

There is the medieval Englishman, activist ('we who are alive'), impatient of dogma, unwilling to be involved in the world-state of sinners, content with the 'City' which is his own community, responsible, rational, humane, but taking orders from nobody whom he does not personally know.

The inwardness of English medieval church history is illuminated by such clues as *Piers Plowman*'s thumbnail-sketch. But about the time that poem was being written a number of sectional and more technical Dissents were being brought to a synthesis in the person and teaching of John Wyclif.

Wyclif's Dissent was of a different order from those sporadic Dissents which preceded him. During the hundred years about 1250–1350 the tempo of Dissent begins to quicken, and outward events begin to converge in a manner that makes a large and dramatic Dissent possible. There was Henry Bracton (d. 1268), the greatest lawyer of his day, who sang in a loud voice the already familiar tune about the State's encroachments on church preserves in matters of law, and transposed it into a key that made it especially audible in Rome as a gesture towards English church-nationalism. There was the philosopher William of Occam (d. 1349), most learned of the Franciscans, who, in defending his order against papal disapproval, was defending the principle of 'orders' in the Church against papal absolutism. There was Richard Fitzralph of Armagh (d. 1360), who took the opposite ground and flayed the degenerate Franciscans with fierce words, denouncing the Papacy for offering them any approval at all. There was Thomas Bradwardine (d. 1349), an evangelical before his time, attacking English Pelagianism in his treatises on conversion, and exhorting the church to a greater holiness than papal example enjoined.

It really begins to appear that the Pope can do nothing right in the eyes of Englishmen; but up to 1349 the voices crying in the wilderness are solitary voices of individual

Dissenters. The year 1349 brought the Black Death, whose social consequences throughout Europe were incalculable, but are probably best seen as paralleled by the social consequences of the two World Wars in the first half of the present century. Misfortune on that scale does not ennoble a continent, even though it may raise the temperature of zeal and adventure and even courage in some. The Jacqueries in France and the Peasants' Revolt in England follow a now familiar pattern of social Dissent; and the climate was made the more favourable to Dissent both social and religious by the difficulties into which during the same period the Papacy had fallen. The papal residence at Avignon (1309–78) and the added scandal of the papal schism (1378–1418) did nothing to preserve in the minds of the people a papal *mystique* that could have made them, especially if they were Englishmen, pause in their reforming zeal and ask questions about their loyalty to Rome.

The religious Dissent corresponding to the social Dissent of the generation following the Black Death is gathered up in Wyclif. And Wyclif is the 'morning star of the Reformation' in as much as he caused an advance in English religious thought on a three-pronged front—patriotism, rationalism and evangelical holiness. He was a patriot, or so he styled himself, as much as Bracton, in that his anti-papal presumptions were based on a conviction that the Pope's writ just did not run in England. He was an apostle of evangelical holiness, just as much as Bradwardine, in that he, and even more his followers the Lollards, protested with violence against clerical laxities and a tendency throughout the hierarchy to lower standards of morality and devotion. And to these characteristic notes of the medieval reformer he added this third note—characteristic of the post-Renaissance Reformer—

that the individual has a right to direct access to the fountain-head of doctrine: to this end, he translated the Bible into English for the first time.

Wyclif's dogmatic contentions do not here concern us. It is sufficient to say, for it is everywhere agreed, that his doctrine of 'Dominion', in which power is closely correlated with merit at all levels, his evangelical doctrines of the Atonement and of personal salvation, his doctrine of the Church as the 'Communion of the Saved', and his attack on Transubstantiation are all the consequence of the fusion in his own mind of the three elements of Reformation—patriotism, rationalism and holiness. Papal absolutism is the target of his patriotism, ecclesiastical obscurantism of his rationalism, and ecclesiastical laxity of his crusade for holiness. And although the Church took what opportunity it could of extinguishing this Dissent in Wyclif's person, the pious, half-educated, Bible-centred zealots who became known as Lollards remained active, often in an underground way, to the propagation of a body of evangelical opinion. The last Lollard was put to death by Henry VIII in 1532. 'Lollard' is a comic word-formation signifying 'mumbler', and symbolizes the Pelagian squire's patronizing contempt for these primitive Bible-bangers. But with all their mumbling, much of which would be equally offensive to a comfortably-born orthodox English Protestant of today, they spoke a very clear word to the English society whose feudal structure was already collapsing.

These, though their activities as recorded seem to have died away about the middle of the fifteenth century, were the real disseminators of that opinion which in Henry VIII's time was waiting for the chance to express itself systematically. It was the last thing that Henry wanted; but it was this evangelical Dissent, this positive reforming mind looking for an English faith, a personal faith, and a rule of holiness based on Scripture, that was in fact let loose when Henry made his final breach with Rome. It was as ready to dissent from Henry as from the Pope. It was ready to dissent from almost anybody, and certainly from any kind of State establishment of religion. Henry's machinations provided the occasion for its emergence as an English institution.

The reader will already be wondering whether his present author proposes to deny any kind of continental roots to English Dissent. Not at all: this is where they must be mentioned. It was the influence and example of Wyclif that caused John Hus, the evangelical Dissenter of Bohemia, to institute a campaign along very much the same broad lines on the Continent, and so to embarrass the Papacy that he suffered violent death at the behest of the Council of Constance in 1415. Hus was another apostle of patriotism and holiness, another 'personal' reader of the Scriptures, and he is the founder of another 'underground' religious movement. The 'Bohemian Brethren' or 'Hussites' or, at a later stage, the Moravian Brotherhood, is probably a good picture of what Lollardy would have been in this country had Henry VIII not done what he did. Moravianism, which is at bottom Hussite, traces its foundation to the year 1457; it has often been persecuted and driven into hiding; and yet at two points—in its contributions to the Lutheran Reformation (chiefly in an activity very dear to Luther's heart, and much dearer than their theology, namely the writing of hymns and sacred ballads) and in its profound influence on John Wesley, it has made vital contributions to the history of Protestantism. It is quite fairly judged by one historian that 'Wyclif was an original genius. Hus is to him as a planet to the sun.'[9] Their agreements in doctrine and exhortation were far more numerous than their divergences. And although Luther held much of the theology of the Hussites in contempt, it was they who did much of the preparation of a soil that could readily receive his word when the time came for it to be spoken.

CHAPTER III

NEW AGE

1. *Medieval Enthusiasm*

The continental background of English Dissent is best described by saying that for at least three centuries before English Dissent became organized and clamorous, people here and there on the Continent had been saying things which Englishmen found, in translation, suitable to their purpose. We are, indeed, in some danger of overloading this introductory part of the book by pressing the principle of Dissent farther and farther back in church history until we reach the days of the twelve Apostles: and there would be a case for doing precisely that, but in another book.

What matters here is that we should make clear what is the origin of that rebellious, truculent accent in Dissent which is one of its most evident characteristics, especially in the English seventeenth century. Therefore we must make some observations on the pre-Renaissance enthusiastic sects, on the Renaissance itself, and on the Anabaptists of the sixteenth century.

There is always a point in the history of any kind of organized Dissent at which it comes near the frontier between what Mr E. J. Hobsbawm in his book *Primitive Rebels* has distinguished as the 'reforming' and the 'revolutionary tempers'.[1] The Reformer, he says, is he who dissents but believes that an existing social (or religious) system can be adjusted or improved to meet his requirements; while the revolutionary is he who must overthrow the existing system and replace it *in toto*. English Dissent, or at any rate orthodox Dissent, has always been of the reforming rather than of the revolutionary kind; but even in English Dissent, and more notably in certain other Dissents which made their contribution to the background of its history, the boundary has been crossed.

A clear parallel to Mr Hobsbawm's distinction between reforming and revolutionary, applicable to continental Dissents, appears in Mgr Ronald Knox's *Enthusiasm*, where he suggests that the best way to find one's way through the jungle of medieval continental sects is to regard them as divided into two groups, the Waldensian and the Catharist (or Albigensian). The fountain-head of the Waldensians (alternatively called Vaudois) was at Lyons, but they soon settled in northern Italy where, after an 'underground' existence comparable to that of the Hussites, they still flourish as a Protestant sect. The Albigensians belonged always to southern France. Quoting H. J. Warner, *The Albigensian Heresy*, Knox wrote, 'the Catharists regarded the church as irremediably corrupt, while the Waldenses cherished the ambition of reforming it'.[2] And although Knox is rightly cautious about making the distinction too firm, it is clear that there was, at any given time anywhere between 1100 and 1400, a Dissenting spirit of reform here, and a Dissenting spirit of rebellion there. The Waldensians on the whole tended towards reform through evangelical holiness and a criticism of the Church's worldliness, while the Albigensians tended on the whole to rebel against all the forms and sacraments of the Church and to invent their own disciplines and forms of worship. In all these movements—Knox provides a list of thirty-five of them and says it is not exhaustive—the marks of religious Dissent are evident: the cult of holiness, a rationalism that, mentally, dislikes being dictated to, and a patriotism that sometimes is reduced to a parochialism.

These have their place in the general scheme of things; but it is especially interesting to attend to one extraordinary figure, the Abbot Joachim of Fiore (d. 1202), whom Hobsbawm quotes Professor Norman Cohn as describing as 'the inventor of the most influential prophetic system known to Europe before the appearance of Karl Marx'.[3] Joachim, himself a cloistered mystic, set down in three published works the theory that history divides itself into three 'ages': the 'age of the Father', which is the age during which mankind lived under the Law, and extended from the beginning of time to the Incarnation; the age of the 'Son', during which mankind lived under New Testament Grace; and the 'age of the Spirit', which was to begin in the year 1260. That year, well in the future at the time when he died, he chose as being forty-two conventional 'generations' (cf. Matt. i. 17) from the Incarnation. The important point to notice is this: that the third age was to be the age in which the New Testament Church would be seen to have finished its work, and in which new religious orders would arise to convert the whole world. Just as 'Grace' was a new dimension after 'Law', so the new 'freedom', which most significantly he describes as of the *Spiritus Intellectus*, would be a new dimension after Grace. No longer a Church divided from the world, a Church instituted as a walled city defending itself against the heathen: no longer this world divided between godly and ungodly, heathen and Christian, but a Church coterminous with the world, whose guiding spirit was the 'Intellectual spirit'.

A strange mixture, this, of conventional biblical-style prophecy and a rationalism that foreshadowed the Renaissance. Joachim set it down on paper and returned to his prayers; but the notion caught the imagination of

men who formed themselves into small bodies calling
themselves the 'Spiritual Franciscans' or the 'Fraticelli',
and, for their somewhat horrific religious practices, known
by others as 'Flagellants'. It was no accident that the
peak year of the Flagellants was 1259.

Here was a real context for enthusiasm amounting to
rebellion. Here was a doctrine of the 'new age' of freedom,
in which not only the old law of the Ten Commandments,
but the new law of the New Testament Church, was done
away. In the minds of the Fraticelli Joachim's doctrines,
in their original version wonderfully complex and wonderfully tentative, simplified themselves into a crude millenarianism. 'A new age is about to begin. Down with the
authorities of the old age. Away with its trappings. Repent
and make yourselves worthy of it. Join us and enjoy it.'
Here were all the fierce austerities, here was the crusading
zealotism, here was the fanatical messianism that today go
with Communism. Here was something for your 'journey-
man apostle' (another good word from Knox) to offer to
people who would hear. Here was especially something
with which to fire the imagination of the malcontents.

In itself it came to little. But as a symptom it is of the
very first importance. It is this 'new age' fanaticism that
provides a ready-made mould into which at the appointed
time the Renaissance can pour its new intellectual plastics.

2. *Renaissance*

It is here, indeed, that we find the path along which we can
approach the notion of 'Renaissance' in a manner most
profitable for our present study. 'Renaissance' as it bears
on Reformation and religious Dissent is primarily the
'new age of the intellect'; historically it is the consequence
of mankind claiming a new kind of intellectual right. It

was, essentially, a full chorus, preceded by a number of introductory solos in different parts of the choir, in which are clearly distinguishable the words 'We will no longer be dictated to'. Renaissance is not an overthrowing of doctrine. It is not anti-clerical or anti-ecclesiastical in itself. That is a proper description of the eighteenth-century *Aufklärung*. But it is a new kind of self-assertion, whose consequences in the arts have been more widely canvassed than its consequences in religious thinking.

But we can refer to art for illustration. What we mean by Renaissance is exemplified in the difference between the muscular, humanly expressive figures in Michelangelo's 'Holy Family' and the draped, formal figures in Giotto's 'Presentation'. It is the difference between the melody-and-accompaniment texture of primitive seventeenth-century Italian opera and the ecclesiastical counterpoint of William Byrd. And music adds a dimension of illustration to what is given by painting. For your typically 'Renaissance' music, with its virtuoso 'tune' and its subservient 'bass' is quite certainly of the new age, whereas the disciplined and yet equal 'conversation' of Tudor counterpoint is of the old age: and yet you see in the new music an unprecedented freedom enjoyed by the soloist at the expense of an unprecedented subservience in the accompaniment or bass. That illustrates the formidable problems that were to confront the society of Europe once the intellectual and political virtuoso claimed freedom at the expense of those who were to be his servants. The fearful paradox of claimed freedom was to replace the discipline of modified freedom. What was always unofficial, disapproved, unorthodox in the feudal system, namely freedom individually claimed, now came out on the surface as one of the rights of man. This was the opportunity for the individually brilliant to make more of himself than he could have done earlier: but this was done, as the appalling social stratification of the eighteenth century in Europe shows, at grievous expense. There is always the danger of romanticizing those Middle Ages which were not self-conscious enough to leave us the kind of documents modern researchers care most for: but there need be no real doubt that the misery of the villages visited by John Wesley was of a different, and surely darker, kind than the misery of the medieval peasantry. Did Hilaire Belloc go too far when he said epigrammatically of the Middle Ages, 'There were no potatoes; but then, there were no suicides'?

The Renaissance, so far as we are now interested in it, was a claim. And Dissent is in part a claim. It is the claim of a deprived group for its rights. It may be an exalted and altruistic claim. It may be a paranoiac whine. It all depends on who is making it and where. But one way or another it is a claim. The age of St Thomas Aquinas, who gathered all knowledge under theology, the Queen of the Sciences, in his *Summa Theologiae*, gives place to the age of Leonardo: monolithic certainties give place to questing brilliance.

3. *Literacy and 'The Word'*

The whole of Europe, by the year 1453, was waiting for the momentous discovery of the first printers. It was printing that crystallized the Renaissance. And printing had more to do with the Reformation than any other historic agency. A Renaissance of individual brilliance in ideas is impressive enough: but the multiplying and communication and cross-fertilizing of these ideas, and their dissemination amongst the people at large, is what is

required to make 'Renaissance' effective. The consequence of printing was, in a few generations, to make books
part of the normal landscape—books and, more especially,
pamphlets. It induced in a large and influential section of
European society a gradually increasing, and later a geo-
metrically increasing, sense of their right to understand,
their right to read; and it is not surprising that the whole of
theology lurches violently to one side because of a sudden
new insight into the whole conception of 'The Word'.

It was from this point that Protestant conceptualism
began to develop quickly, and it took many forms—a viru-
lent antipathy to images of any visible kind, and to the use
in religious practice of the faculty of imagination; a new
literalism in the interpretation of Scripture; a new cult of
'the simple', meaning what was openly intelligible; an
insistence on the right of the ordinary worshipper to
understand the words and acts of the priest, and of the
ordinary man to work out his own religion; an insistence
on vernacular Bibles; a new form of 'argued' theology,
brought to its greatest height in the *Institutes* of John
Calvin. Add together the various forces that have begun
to be at work for the unseating of the ancient medieval
tradition, and this is the resultant they produce: a suspicion of human authority, a suspicion of what is not to
be fully stated in the black and white of print and paper, a
tendency to emphasize local nationalisms and to make the
vernacular a symbol of retreat from metropolitan language
and culture, and a strong movement towards personal
religion and holiness and away from the institutional. In
other words, patriotism, rationalism and evangelical holiness plus a touch of rebellion, which is what we get most
simply by adding Wyclif's theology to the social temper of
the Peasants' Revolt.

29

4. *Anabaptism*

Anabaptism is a very complete example of this. 'Anabaptists' is a compendious term for a number of sixteenth-century movements on the Continent which shared a violently enthusiastic temper and a reforming piety which was at some points virtually revolutionary. Their name implies that they insisted on the practice of adult baptism, an insistence which has its root in the assumption that the believer's ability to understand is an inseparable part of faith. Adult baptism is a characteristic symptom of the 'claim' of the new age; it is ultimately a gesture of claim, not of acceptance. Among the Anabaptist groups were the followers of Thomas Muntzer (d. 1525) who made themselves heard in Wittenburg in 1521, the Swiss believers of Zurich (1525), the Hutterians of Moravia, the Hoffmanites of Holland, and the followers of Jan Mattys and Jan Bockelson in Holland, who ultimately organized themselves into the denomination now known as the Mennonites. It is difficult to open a page of Anabaptist writing without encountering some ferocious denunciation of the Catholic Church, some wild chiliastic frenzy, or some picturesquely worded assertion that man is now delivered from the bondage of the Middle Ages. A short passage from Muntzer's Sermon before the Princes will serve:

One sees nicely how the eels and vipers all in a heap abandon themselves to obscenities. The priests and all the wicked clerics are the vipers, as John the Baptist calls them, and the temporal lords and princes are the eels, as is figuratively presented in Leviticus (ii. 10–13). For the kingdoms of the devil have smeared themselves with clay. O beloved lords, how handsomely the Lord will go smashing among the old pots with his rod of iron! (Ps. ii. 9).[4]

Dietrich Philips in his treatise on *The Church of God* (c. 1560) expresses in stark fundamentalist terms the new doctrine at its crudest—the primacy of the 'Sacred Word of God' literally taken, the necessity of keeping the congregation of believers pure by instituting 'evangelical separation' (i.e. local excommunication), the duty of Christian believers to practise the highest possible moral precepts on New Testament lines, and the duty of Christians to accept persecution at the world's hands, and even to invite it. His description of the Church is typical: 'All things have been made new through Jesus Christ; the oldness of the letter and of the flesh has passed away, and the upright new being of the Spirit has been ushered in by Jesus Christ.... The impure and the liars shall not enter into this holy city.'

Anabaptism was full of martyrs; by temperament, Anabaptists seem to have looked for martyrdom. They pleased nobody. They pleased Luther, Zwingli and Calvin hardly better than they pleased the Pope. Their courage was boundless, their capacity for offending both disciplinarians and theologians, Catholic and Protestant, astonishing. Muntzer and Philips are, for Anabaptists, moderate. The outer fringes of Anabaptism looked for a world in which the Commandments were entirely abrogated. When it came, as it did here and there, to serious recommendations of polygamy, there was no hope whatever of their carrying the rest of the world with them; but even their out-and-out pacifism was of an anti-social rather than a benevolent kind.

What Anabaptism did bring to the foreground, however, was the notion of 'God-enjoined separatism', that is, of a complete divorce between the Church and the world. For them, any kind of compromise with State authority was compromise with the world, and any importation of secular political values into the Church in the shape of orders and authorities was a corruption. You are told, they said, by the First Epistle of John to hate the world. The State is the world, therefore you must have no truck with it.

Dr George H. Williams, the Harvard historian, makes an illuminating comment on Anabaptism, which can be spread over the whole field of radical or revolutionary reformation. He distinguishes between the 'backward-looking' stream of thought, which proclaimed that the Church must 'go back to the Bible', and the 'forward-looking' stream, which insists above all on preparation for membership of a new age and a new society.[5] Distinct from both are 'the established and protected churches, both Protestant and Catholic, which were, so to speak, churches of the exigent present, and therefore disposed to compromise and accommodation'.[6] That wise comment shows us from another angle the new literal-primitivism and the chiliasm of the reforming enthusiasts, which in the less educated of them are separated with reckless irresponsibility, but in the more theologically minded of them are fused with an ingenuity that always owes much to the biblical imagery of the apocalyptic prophets and the Book of Revelation.

Anabaptism was the fiercest and the most-martyred of all the continental reforming parties, and it represents an extreme form of Dissent. Here the adjectives 'pathological' and 'paranoiac' are often not too strong. And Anabaptism is linked with English Lollardy in a characteristically trenchant epigram by Professor Gordon Rupp, who wrote, 'In the high matter of the Sacrament of the Altar, new Anabaptist was but old Lollard writ Dutch'. In more matters than that exalted one, there was sympathy between Lollardy and Anabaptism. What took fire among continental Anabaptists, and remained something of an eccentricity, took fire here

1   John Wyclif

in þe chirche/ firste apostlis· þe se
counde tyme prophetis· þe þridde
techers· aftirþuarde vertues· aftir
þuarde graces of helyngis· helpyn
gis· gouernaylis or gouernynges
kyndis of langagis· interpretaci
ouns of þhordis /þher alle ben a
postlis / þher alle prophetis· /þher
alle techers· /þher alle vertues· /
þher alle men haue grace of
helyngis· /þher alle quoken þhiþ
langagis· /þher alle interpretæ
or expounen · forsoþe sue zee
þe better goodly ziftis· and zit
/ þhelbe to zou anoþer excellent
or þhortir þeye / — // — // —

IF / ſpeke þhiþ tungis
of men · & aungelis· forſoþly
/ haue no charite· / am
made as braſſe sounyng·
or a cymbal tynkynge· and zif /
haue prophecye·/& haue knoþen
alle mysteries & al kunnynge·
or science· /& zif / haue al feiþ· ſo
þat / ouerbere hillis fro a place
into anoþer· forſoþe zif / ſhal
not haue charite· / am nouzt
and zif / ſhal departe alle my
goodis into metis of pore men·
& zif / ſhal bitake my body· ſo þat
/ brenne· forſoþe zif / ſhal not
haue charite· it profitiþ to me
no þing/ charite is pacient/ it
is benygne· or of good þille·
charite enuyeþ not· it doiþ not
gile· it is not inblolben þhiþ pri
It is not ambicious or coueytous
of þhorſhipis· it ſeekiþ not þo þin
gis þat ben heir oþne· it is not
ſtirede to þrayþe· it þenkiþ
not euyl· it ioyeþ not on þicki
d
nesse· forſoþe it ioyeþ ... to gi
dir· to treuþe· it ſuffriþ alle þin
gis· it bileueþ alle þingis· it ho
piþ alle þingis· it ſuſteyneþ
alle þingis/ charite falliþ not
doune· þheyer prophecies ſhulen
be voydide· oþer langagis ſhuleñ

cese· oþer science ſhal be diſtruyede
forſoþe of partie þhee haue knoþen
and of partie þhe prophecien· forſo
þe þhanne þat ſhal come þat is
parfite· þat þing þat is of partie
ſhal be avoydide /þhanne / þas
a litil childe· / ſpac as a litil childe·
/ vndirſtode as a litil childe forſoþe
þhanne / þas made a man· · /
voydide þo þingis þat þeren of
a litil childe / forſoþe þe ſeen noli
by a myrour in dirkneſſe· þanne
forſoþe face to face· noli / knolþe
of partie· þanne forſoþe / ſhal
knolþe· as / am knolben· noli
forſoþe dþellen þeiþ hope· charite
yes· þre· forſoþe þe more of hem
is charite // — // — // — /c · 16

SUE zee charite· loue zee
ſpiritual þingis· more
forſoþe þat zee prophecie·
forſoþe he þat ſpekiþ in
tunge· ſpekiþ not to men but
to god· forſoþe no man heriþ/ ſo þe
ly þe ſpirit ſpekiþ mysteries·
forſoþ he þat prophecieþ· ſpekiþ
to men to edificacioñ / moneſtyng
& coumfortyng· he þat ſpekiþ in
tunge· edifieþ hym ſelf· forſoþe
he þat prophecieþ· edifieþ þe chir
che of god forſoþe / þole zou alle
forto ſpeke in tungis· but more
forto prophecye· forſoþ he þat
prophecieþ· is more þan he þat
ſpekiþ in tungis or langagis · no
but parauenture he interprete
or declare· þat þe chirche take edi
ficacioñ· ſtolþe forſoþe breþeren
zif / ſhal come to zou ſpekynge
in tungis· þhat ſhal / prophetæ
profite· nobut zif / ſhal ſpeke
to zou oþer in reuelacioun oþer
in science· oþer in prophecie· oþer
in techynge· nepeles þo þingis
þat ben þhiþ outen ſoule or lijf
zyuynge· voyces· oþer pipe· oþer
harpe· nobut zif þei ſhuleñ
zyue diſtynccioñ of ſounyngis·

at home among those whom John Foxe called 'the secret multitude of true professors', and who were among those 'known men' who presented so intractable a problem to Wolsey, Thomas Cromwell, and More.[7]

These, then, thus briefly recounted but to be fully read of in the histories and source-books now available, were the movements which provided the climate in which English religious Dissent began. What this Dissent owes to the major continental Reformers is superficial compared with what it owed to the kind of opinion that was being disseminated by the Renaissance enthusiasts. It was all very well for the English theologians to take what they could from Luther, to drink deep of Calvin on Church Order and the irresistibility of Grace. The people behind the leaders were less interested in Luther and Calvin than in the satisfaction of grievances of which they had been made conscious by much subtler and less evident agencies. The early English Dissenting preacher did not preach Luther and Calvin. He preached the Gospel—and he gathered his congregation by preaching it as a Gospel which would satisfy claims they were quite sure were legitimate. It was a Gospel of controversy, not of peace, of claim, not of acceptance. As preached by even the mighty ones, let alone the small fry, it was full of magnificent inconsistencies. The polity that came from it, as advocated by these same devoted men, was a marvellous amalgam of evangelical perfectionism with crude spiritual cupidity. But these were human beings living in a turbulent and brilliant and free-speaking age, an age when human life went cheap and the tempers of rulers were short; there never was an age in respect of which an historian is more thankful that it is no business of his to judge morally between the two, four or ten parties to any given dispute.

CHAPTER IV

PRIMITIVE AXIOMS

1. *Church and State*

In the year of Henry VIII's final breach with the Papacy, this country was ready for an explosion of Dissent. Once Henry had cut off the country from formal Catholic allegiance, it remained to be seen what form the English Church should take. On this there were many opinions, diversified into complicated subdivisions. But broadly it came to this: that on the one hand there were those who hoped for the best from the new State Church, while on the other there were those who found it a more disastrous notion than they had found formal Catholicism.

Everything depended on whether, at your best, you believed that the Church and the State were two authorities which must cross-fertilize each other, that both were ordained by God towards the same ultimate purpose. If this was your belief, you were bound to attach plenty of importance to the State's function in church affairs. It was positively agreeable to this belief that the sovereign, *qua* sovereign, should be recognized as an authority in the Church. Not only was there no reason why bishops should not be appointed by the Crown; it was good that they should be so appointed, even though you believed that the Crown had better take the right advice before making the appointments. If in your view the State is the people at work, and the Church the same people at prayer, then the Church must allow for the Head of the State to take his place in the government of the spiritualities: and conversely the State must tolerate authoritative direction in certain matters from the Lords Spiritual.

At your worst, of course, you might see some personal advantage in supporting the new Establishment which there was nothing to be gained, and much to be lost, by repudiating. But this generalized belief in the interplay of Church and State as spiritual and legislative authorities is accepted by all those who accept certain familiar features of modern English life. There is room in the House of Lords for certain bishops; the Crown retains the gift of certain livings and university Chairs and the right to appoint the higher officers of the Church of England; and if these appear to some Dissenting minds to be matters requiring criticism and adjustment, it was very difficult for most people to be Puritan enough to be unimpressed by the interplay of authorities and obediences that was religiously dramatized in the coronation of our present Queen. The ideal symbolized in the bowing of the Queen before the archbishop, and of the archbishop before the Queen, represents the most agreeable aspect of the opinion that Church and State need each other and can be friends. None the less for that, history insists that we judge this ideal to be easily seen by men of the twentieth century only because the controversy between Church and State was worked out with such fierce zeal on both sides in days when ideals were much less easy to see, and when the practicalities were much more insistent for solution. It is quite impossible to read back into the situation of 1562 the associations that our monarchy now has for most Englishmen. Something has historically happened to the monarchy, and something has historically happened to the English episcopate, which removes from the scene most of the causes for violent antipathy that prevailed in the sixteenth century. It is part of my present business to explain just what has happened. But it is enough for the moment to imagine the difference between what the ordinary middle-of-the road Anglican thinks about monarchy and episcopacy today, and what he thought of them in 1562. It is enough to recall that the English Reformation was brought into being, as an act of State, by that astounding mixture of folly, virility, generosity, unscrupulousness, obstinacy and personal magnetism, Henry VIII, that his successor spent most of his brief reign as a minor under unofficial regents, and that Queen Mary sought by violence to reverse the whole process of the English Reformation. There was no reason why in 1562 the ordinary Anglican should trust the monarchy. There was every reason for the time-server to profess allegiance, but this is a very different thing from the kind of allegiance and trust that on the whole bind the people to the Crown in our own time.

Therefore, after Mary's reign, there was a large body of Dissent, and there were many who on principle suspected either this queen as holding power in the Church, or any State-authority as holding such power. Dissent divided itself, once again, into the reforming and the revolutionary, the 'anglican' Puritan and the 'separatist' Puritan.

2. *War on images*

As an example of the line taken by non-separatist reforming opinion against those who by now could be called conservative Anglicans, take the representations made by the 'Puritan' party in the Convocation of 1562. (It was the publication of these that first led, in 1564, to the half-derisive coinage of the word 'Puritan'.)

Among other matters, they proposed certain modifications in the conduct of public worship enjoined in the 1549 and 1552 Prayer Books: that the observance of 'Holy Days' (other than Christmas, Easter, Whitsun and all Sundays) be abolished; that the parish minister should say the service, even when he is at the altar, facing the people, 'that the people may be edified'; that at Baptism the sign of the Cross be omitted; that no vestments apart from the surplice be permitted in church; that kneeling at Communion be a matter of private judgement, not of obligation; and that organs be removed from all churches.

There we see at once a cult of 'Gospel simplicity' which springs straight from those Dissents we have already encountered. All these requirements can be brought under one of the three heads of Reformation—that of 'rationalism'. It can here be subdivided into suspicion of images, and adherence to scriptural precept. This was a typical claim of the Reformation.

Much of medieval religion was a matter of images. It had to be. Nobody but clergy and lawyers could read, and what the worshipper saw, smelt, and (musically) heard were the chief means by which the Gospel was communicated to him. As one modern historian has said, 'The church itself was the common man's service book'— images of the saints, stained-glass windows, dramatic movements by priest and congregation during the celebration of the Mass: these were the means, more potent than the actual words of liturgy or even of sermon, by which the truth met his affections and his mind.

It is only when the ugly word 'superstition' becomes current as a description of what happened in the medieval worshipper's mind that a new line of thought is set in train. Renaissance man, Puritan man, Dissenting English man, was in a new way sensitive; he was sensitive not now to the impact of images on his imagination, but to the

necessity of seeing that his neighbour used his mind
rightly. So he became suspicious of all the drama and
choreography and orchestration of the Mass as being
enemies of man's conceptual faculty. 'That the people
may be edified' is the key phrase. Let the service be said
plainly and in English: let dramatic movements of the
priest's hands and the worshipper's knees be discouraged;
let colour be abolished from the priest's dress and all but
the plainest congregational unison music be done out of
the churches. Then—it is clearly implied—we shall have
an intelligible, un-hypocritical, un-superstitious, clean-
living religion of which Englishmen can be proud.

It is as necessary for Catholics as for Dissenters to
understand just how remarkable this contention would
have appeared to a medieval friar or priest. In English
religious life nowadays it is a commonplace. Even English
Catholics are looking for a vernacular liturgy. But it is
a post-Renaissance commonplace. No medieval church,
except the abbeys of certain preaching orders, was so built
that the speaking voice of a priest might be heard. It was
built as a visual aid to the people's devotion, on a large
scale compared with the needs of the local population, to
symbolize the length and breadth and (especially) height
of the subject to which it was dedicated: magnificently
trans-utilitarian, eloquent of the primacy of love over
gain in the dimensions of the Kingdom. Dissent, however,
pours cold water on the awed reaction of the medieval-
minded to all this. The Puritan drops the words 'superstition' or 'sentimentality' into the conversation, and at
once the spell is broken. Puritans have no use at all for
spells. But no Dissenter will be a decent historian, or a
good ecumenical Christian, until he has learnt what a
Catholic or Anglican layman means when he makes the (to

him) outrageous statement, 'but it doesn't matter whether you can hear or not'. To the loyal Dissenting mind this is profanity; it touches an unquestioned axiom (which to touch is like touching a hidden nerve), that the mind is the vital faculty to which the affections must always be subordinated.

So much by way of comment on the 1562 Convocation. But before we encounter the first overt signs of separatism, we must make one further comment. It concerns a new category which English Puritanism used to interpret the older category of patriotism: namely, freedom.

3. *War on bondage*

There can be no doubt of the dominical authenticity of the demand that it is man's duty to grow up. The passage about 'becoming as little children' in Mark x and Matthew xviii must never be interpreted as placing an evangelical premium on childishness. There is a psychological condition known to the medical specialists as 'infantilism', which causes its subject to be unwilling to take the responsibilities of maturity, and to seek to remain, as much as he can, a partaker of the privileges of childhood. From this condition spring certain aspects of cowardice and sloth, such as uxoriousness, fear of the unknown, lack of initiative, and over-reliance on the judgement and instruction of others. Above all that condition produces a certain misinterpretation of the nature of 'obedience', and a person suffering from it never sees 'obedience' as anything more than a passive submission to unquestioned instructions. The disease does not render its sufferer immune from resentment against the author of the instructions, and for that reason its subject is often in a pitiable state.

Now Puritanism, that is, the extreme form of English

religious Dissent, was always a gesture against this condition. Puritan zeal fairly often attributed the condition to
people who did not suffer from it, and very often showed
itself capable of diagnosing only one cause for any kind of
religious disorder. But allowing for that, the Puritans saw
this condition, as it were, transferred from a society to
a Church. Modern society happens to provide certain
political parallels which are, to be sure, more unam-
biguously of this kind than we can be sure that the English
sixteenth century was. But if you are persuaded that a
society is being kept childish, kept unduly in pupil-status
by its rulers, there are two moral propositions which you
have to establish. The first is that it is a crime against human
personality to keep people from the privilege and respon-
sibility of growing up, even when that crime is disguised
under a series of apparently benevolent gestures. The
second is that it is equally a crime to accept this from
a ruler, and especially a crime to accept his delusive
benevolences.

This is familiar doctrine, and provides the best approach
to the Puritan mind for mid-twentieth-century Englishmen. Mr George Orwell's message in his book *1984* was
clearly based on these two moral propositions. Big Brother
is a criminal even in his benevolences: but you, says the
prophet Orwell to his reader, are hardly less a criminal for
allowing and accepting this kind of thing. Englishmen, but
more especially Americans, feel this way about Soviet
Communism. The moralism of the late John Foster Dulles,
American Secretary of State, was a passionate assertion of
the double proposition: Soviet Communism is a crime,
and equally your acceptance of its benevolences, your
attempts to compromise with it, are a crime. Or again, the
horrifying perplexities of the racial situation in South

Africa and the Southern States of the U.S.A. show us that the coloured peoples are taking the same line about the white races. 'They are criminals', say the coloured peoples, 'and if you accept their gifts you are compromising with them.'

That was the Puritan line, and it was in general the Reformed line, on metropolitan Catholicism. They resisted the Papacy because it was in their eyes a spiritual despotism, and they were prepared to turn their backs on all those aspects of the medieval culture which appear to us to be gracious. They may well have appeared gracious to them. But they were signs of the benevolence with which Big Brother had hoodwinked his subjects. Therefore, although they were gracious, and precisely because they were attractive, they must be set aside. This, I believe, disposes of all those aspects of Puritan austerity towards art and what one might call the public good manners of liturgy whose prohibition does not appear to be derived direct from their theology or from scripture. There is nothing in the New Testament forbidding coloured vestments or organs or stained-glass windows or choirs; there are positive injunctions towards spiritual healing and sacramental anointing, with which the Puritans would have nothing to do. What mattered to them was to make their claim against the Pope, saying 'You are preventing men from growing up', and urging on the people the demand, 'You must not accept this'. Since the direction of this 'growing up' happened, historically, to be so largely intellectual, it was in conceptual terms that they made their claims. The mind, then, must be enthroned over the affections, and the imagination must be sternly censored that it may not corrupt the intellect.

It may here be remarked that had the Council of Trent

really addressed itself to this claim instead of spending all its time on answering the Dissenting claim about 'holiness', history might have taken a different turn. As it happened in fact, after an extraordinarily dilatory start, the Council of Trent took twenty-five years (1538–63) to come to certain conclusions about liturgy, about Catholic sacramental doctrine, about the Reformed doctrine of Justification by Faith, and about Episcopal Residence, the Index, church order, and the offering of the Communion Cup to the people. All these were matters in respect of which the Catholic Church stood in need of internal discipline: but nowhere in the proceedings of the Council do we find any evidence that its members were aware of the real heart of the Reformed claim. Especially do we note its absence where the Council dealt with that doctrine of Justification by Faith which is its classic theological expression.

It might well be too much to insist that the Puritans ever saw their claim in just these terms. It would probably have required supreme human insight in the Catholics to recognize that this was what was being said. But that it was being said there can be no doubt as soon as we observe what began to happen in the English churches.

4. *The primacy of Scripture*

At any rate, the assumption in England was that any Christian must be treated as grown-up enough to read his Bible. The early years of the reign of Queen Elizabeth I show a clear cleavage within the Church of England, between those who adhered to the principles that were to be embodied in the Elizabethan Settlement of 1570 and those who contested them. Here it is the scriptural emphasis that predominates; here is, ex-hypothesi, no rebellion. But the appeal to 'the primitive' suggests strongly the anti-medievalism of the Puritan mind, and that to the Scriptures suggests the rationalistic claim. Let Bishop Jewel of Salisbury (1522–71) speak for himself.

We truly for our parts, as we have said, have done nothing in altering religion either upon rashness or arrogancy; nor nothing but with good leisure and great consideration. Neither had we ever intended to do it, except both the manifest and most assured will of God, opened to us in His Holy Scriptures, and the regard of our own salvation, had even constrained us thereunto. For though we have departed from that Church which these men call Catholic, and by that means get us envy amongst them that want skill to judge, yet is this enough for us, and ought to be enough for every wise and good man, and one that maketh account of ever-lasting life, that we have gone from that Church which had power to err; which Christ, who cannot err, told so long before it could err; and which we ourselves did evidently see with our eyes to have gone both from the holy fathers, and from the Apostles, and from Christ his own self, and from the primitive and Catholic Church and we are come as near as we possibly could to the Church of the Apostles and of the old Catholic bishops and fathers; which Church we know hath hereunto been sound and perfect, and, as Tertullian termeth it, a pure virgin, spotted as yet with no idolatry, nor with any foul or shameful fault: and have directed, according to their customs and ordinances, not only for our doctrine, but also the Sacraments and the form of Common Prayer.[1]

That is a good example of the 'moderate Puritan' view. Let us have a Book of Common Prayer, but let it be reformed, and let our practices be reformed in accordance with the Scriptures and the Fathers.

All the leaders of moderate Dissenting thought at this time were church historians and patristic scholars, and the familiar Anglican emphasis on the first five centuries of church history, still reflected in the requirements for degrees in theology at the ancient English universities, have their origin in the new cult of the Fathers by those who were driven back to them by their revulsion from medieval developments.

But what is of more significance, for it is to be found in the writings of all church controversialists of the English Reformation, is the attitude to the Scriptures, a comment on which must be our last general observation before we begin on the history of the Dissenting interest in England.

It will be observed throughout the early stages of the story we are about to tell, that the Puritan mind insisted that the Scriptures were the only authority to which any man could look for guidance in matters of church order and of Christian behaviour. This doctrine is one which to many modern minds appears blameless; for there is, clearly, a sense in which the Scriptures are a primary authority for all Christians. But as expounded by many of the Puritans the doctrine is far from blameless, and this was observed by no less an authority than Richard Hooker. The Puritan contention always was that the traditions alike of Roman Catholicism and of the nascent Anglicanism added to the pure doctrine of Scripture, and were therefore to be blamed. But Hooker answers as follows:

They which first gave out, that 'nothing ought to be established in the Church which is not commanded by the word of God' thought this principle plainly warranted by the manifest words of the Law, 'Ye shall put nothing into the word which I command you, neither shall you take aught therefrom, that ye may keep the commandments of the Lord your God, which I command you' (Deut. iv. 2 and xii. 32). Wherefore having an eye to a number of rites and orders in the Church of England, as marrying with a ring, crossing in the one sacrament, and kneeling at the other, observing of festival days more than only that which is called the Lord's day, enjoining abstinence at certain times from some kinds of meat, churching of women after childbirth, degrees taken by divines in universities, sundry church offices, dignities and callings, for which they found no commandment in Holy Scripture, they thought by the one stroke of that axiom to have cut them off.

44

But that which they took for an oracle being sifted was repelled. True it is concerning the word of God, whether it be by misconstruction of the sense or by falsification of the words, wittingly to endeavour that any thing may seem divine which is not, or anything not seem which is, were plainly to abuse, and even to falsify divine evidence; which injury offered but unto men, is most worthily counted heinous. Which point I wish they did well observe, with whom nothing is more familiar than to plead in these causes 'the law of God', 'the Word of the Lord'; who notwithstanding when they come to allege what word and what law they mean, their common ordinary practice is to quote by-speeches in some historical narration or other, and to urge them as if they were written in most exact form of law. What is to add to the law of God, if this be not? When that which the word of God doth but deliver historically we construe without any warrant as if it were legally meant, and so urge it further than we can prove that it was intended; do we not add to the laws of God, and make them in number seem more than they are? It standeth us to be careful in this case.[2]

Separated from Hooker by 350 years and a whole world of tradition, Paul Tillich wrote to somewhat the same effect:

The recently influential theology of 'the Word' should be careful not to confuse the divine 'Word', which has appeared as a personal life and is the *Gestalt* of grace, with the biblical or ecclesiastical word. For Christian theology Jesus the Christ is the Word (i.e. the divine self-manifestation); and this involves his being in its totality, to which his deeds and his suffering belong, and not his words alone. 'Word of God' in Christian theology, therefore, has an obviously symbolic sense.[3]

Scripture literally interpreted, Scripture's silences taken as prohibitions and its records taken indiscriminately as injunctions, often appear to be a formidable weapon to those who admit a reverence for the Bible. But it is in fact a bad weapon, and the historian's business here is to note that in 1560 it was a new weapon.

Vernacular Bibles were part of the total Dissenting claim. But given your vernacular Bible, what assurance have you that you will be given understanding of it? To be sure, very little, if you are in a situation of essential haste, impatience and polemic such as that in which the early Puritans found themselves. They were slow to recognize (and they are not much to be blamed: many Christians have not yet admitted it) that the the proper handling of a vernacular Bible involves the willingness and ability to distinguish between one kind of literature and another, and the readiness to accept that plain factual statement and direct universal injunction are not the only means by which historic and moral truth are communicated through literature. This the primitive Dissenters did not stop to consider. The tragedy was that there were very few men of the ability of Hooker who could point out the flaw in their reasoning. Nobody in that age refuted the 'the Bible says' argument with such patience and reasonableness as Hooker did in his third Book.

The word 'tragedy' is hardly too strong. Enormous blocks of the structure of Puritan faith and practice were built up on the 'the Bible says' foundation. The proper answer was, and is, 'that is not the way to read the Bible'. The answer supplied by Catholics to Reformers, and by the High Churchmen to the Dissenters, was in other terms —ecclesiastical here, political there: appeal was made to the necessities of keeping the peace, to the security laws, to the divine right of sovereign or bishops, to the good nature of the Dissenters, to the doctrines of the Fathers, to anything but the real authority of the Bible, which lay elsewhere than where either High Churchman or Puritan was looking for it.

For it must never be forgotten that the Bible was written in Hebrew and in Greek, and that even an ability to translate from those languages affords no certainty that a reader will grasp its meaning sufficiently to be able to deduce its moral and practical demands for any particular age. It was too easy for men either to treat the vernacular Bible as though it were written in English for Englishmen (or in German for Germans), or, where they had better learning, to treat it as a classic source-book for canon law. The same movement of the Western spirit that produced the Renaissance produced both the Dissents that make the pattern of the Reformation, and the vernacular Bibles which were their text-books. But in the earliest years of controversy it became very plain that the vernacular Bible was to prove the source not of reconciliation but of deeper and more painful controversy. It could not have been otherwise, and it has remained so into our own time.

CHAPTER V

FIRST STEPS, 1567–93

1. *Plumbers' Hall*

On the nineteenth of June 1567, the sheriffs of the City of London paid an official visit to the Plumbers' Hall. There they found about a hundred people holding a religious service. Representatives of this congregation, with their minister, were arrested, and after a night in the cells they appeared before the Lord Mayor of London, the Bishop of London (Edmund Grindal), and other officers. This was the first recorded instance of a separatist congregation in England after the Reformation, and is usually regarded as the first emergence in this country of what is now known as Congregationalism.

In answer to the remonstrances of the Bishop and the Dean of Westminster, these separatists urged their objections to 'the use of surplices and copes in the Church', which they styled 'idolatrous gear'; this objection, they claimed, the 'prince' (that is, Queen Elizabeth I, who was still styled the 'supreme head' of the English Church) had no power to make them withdraw.

Their argument at its simplest has therefore two limbs: an objection to certain specific customs in the Church of England, and a defiance of the sovereign's authority to make them conform. No doubt it is as difficult for a modern Englishman to conceive a congregation deliberately separating itself from the Church of England on so apparently trifling an issue as that of vestments, as it is to imagine any justification for the authorities' imprisoning the objectors for nonconformity. But to attend

3 Latimer and Ridley at the stake

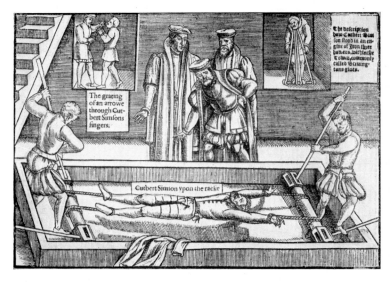

4*a* Cuthbert Simson on the rack
(from Foxe's *Booke of Martyrs*)

4*b* The burning of Rose Allin's hand
(from Foxe's *Booke of Martyrs*)

church was still the law of the land, and no provision was made in that law for any church but the Church of England. Therefore the separatist congregation had committed a technical breach of the law. But beneath the superficialities of this Dissent was a Lollard-like conviction that in handing over the headship of the English Church to the sovereign the Church had done a blasphemous thing.

It was in the following year that in a letter to Johann Heinrich Bullinger, the Swiss Reformer, Bishop Grindal mentioned a secret church in London, and it is now known that the minister of this congregation was one Richard Fitz. Three contemporary documents bear witness of this gathering. The first, printed in black letter and signed by Fitz himself, sets out three reasons for their separation:

First and foremost, the glorious word and Evangel preached, not in bondage and subjection, but freely and purely. Secondly, to have the Sacraments administered purely only and altogether according to the institution and good word of the Lord Jesus, without any tradition or invention of man: and last of all, to have not the filthy canon law, but discipline only and altogether agreeable to the same heavenly and Almighty Word of our good Lord Jesus Christ.[1]

The second document (in manuscript, signed by twenty-seven members of the congregation and dated 1571) contains this sentence:

We [are] a poor congregation whom God hath separated from the Church of England, and from the mingled and false worshipping therein, out of the which assemblies the Lord our only Saviour hath called us, and still calleth, saying 'Come out from among them, and separate yourselves from them, and touch no unclean thing, then will I receive you, and I will be your God...'.

The third[2] is along the same lines. We hear the authentic Dissenting note at once. Lollard-like humility, Lollard-like striving for holiness: an insistence on the 'purity' of preaching—that is (as always) on the authority of

Scripture literally and rationalistically interpreted: and, when pressed (as they subsequently were), there is a quasi-patriotic insistence on separation, for the nation's sake, from Romish and heathen practices. The phrase 'filthy canon law', which sounds, I suspect, more offensive now than it would have sounded then, for it was an age of uninhibited speech, conceals that revivalistic hatred of the 'legal' which comes direct from Anabaptism. The word was almost certainly put into the writer's mind by the biblical phrase 'your righteousness is as filthy rags', and is meant to symbolize the difference between that obedience to canon law which they attributed to the Anglicans as a mark of churchmanship, and that 'Gospel freedom', which they intended should be the mark of the new church. 'Canon law' stank to their nostrils of that *status pupillaris* in whose bondage Rome had in their view held Europe until the Reformers came.

This pioneer of Dissent, Richard Fitz, is thus a good source for the authentic Dissenting principle in speech and practice. His congregation 'went underground' again, and we do not know what became of him. But he is mentioned in a document of 1593, in Ainsworth's *Counter-poyson* of 1608, and (though not by name, but as part of his church) by John Robinson in 1620. A beginning had been made.

About the time when Fitz was making his brief appearance as a public figure, the Elizabethan Settlement was concluded and published. Upon this, the fruit of more than a decade of consultation and debate, Puritan opinion had much to say. This opinion expressed itself very largely in those polemical pamphlets which are our best source for the Dissenting mind of the time. The earliest of these was printed in late 1572 or early 1573 in the form of an 'Admonition', demanding a review of the Settlement under the familiar heads, but paying special attention to the 'holiness' category. Appealing to the practice of the primitive church, its author contrasts the trial of priests 'for their ability to instruct, and of their godly conversation also' with the modern practice according to which 'by the letters commendatory of some one man, noble or other, tag and rag, learned and unlearned, of the basest sort of the people...are freely received'.[3] The farthest distance to which the English Church has gone from this holy primitiveness is in its admission of prelacy, and of the supreme governorship of the sovereign. (That 'Governor' had been substituted under the Elizabethan Settlement for Henry VIII's 'Head' mattered nothing to them.)

In the primitive church of the New Testament, they go on to say,

Then, as God gave utterance they preached the word only: now they read homilies, articles, injunctions &c. Then, it was painful: now, gainful. Then, poor and ignominious: now, rich and glorious.... Then, ministers were not tied to any form of prayers invented by man, but as the spirit moved them, so they poured forth heart supplications to the Lord. Now they are bound of necessity to a prescript order of service, and book of common prayer in which a great number of things contrary to God's word are contained.[3]

(A footnote at the words 'prescript order' reads, 'Damasus the first inventor of this stuffe. Well furthered by Gregory the 7.')

An unlearned and slothful ministry was to them the worst of scandals; but they had something to say about liturgies, vestments, and the power of the magistracy in administering church matters. This secretly printed pamphlet was widely dispersed, and a second edition was called for. It was accompanied by a tract entitled *A View of*

Popish Abuses, which in some detail enumerated the Puritan complaints against the Church. 'In all their order of service, there is no edification, according to the rule of the Apostle, but confusion; they toss the Psalms in most places like tennis-balls.'[4]

A few years later there appeared a second *Admonition*, whose author was Thomas Cartwright (1535–1603), who had recently (1570) been deprived of the Lady Margaret Chair of Divinity at Cambridge for his outspoken expression of Puritan views. Less trenchant than the former, it devotes much space to the elaboration of the Puritan complaint against bishops. They are accused of sycophancy and of every possible variety of social affectation, and the whole system of patronage is once again attacked. It is, in the Puritan view, the parishioners who should choose their minister, and that priests be 'intruded' into benefices on the recommendation of bishops or courtiers is to him an abomination. 'None have what he (the bishop) may have, except certain fat fellows, with long bags at their girdles, and . . . a dish of Mr Latimer's apples.'[5]

2. *Robert Browne*

And so we come to that stormy and bewildered character who, if we discount the 'underground' movement of Fitz and his congregation, stands as the father of organized English Dissent, Robert Browne. Browne, as his story shows, was Dissent incarnate. Nobody could have been more fittingly chosen to bring Dissent to a national issue.

Browne is supposed, in default of any positive evidence, to have been born about 1550. Our first historic knowledge of him comes when as a (presumably) young Anglican cleric he is invited to preach at St Bennet's (now called St Bene't's), Cambridge. This 'preaching', as he says, was not a settled ministry. 'Whosoever would take charge of them', he says, referring to the congregation there, 'must also come into bondage with them.'[6] A settled ministry within the Church of England was already, to him, a 'bondage'. He confesses that he 'openly preached against the calling and authorizing of preachers by bishops'. This was in 1579. Early in 1580 (new style), he was inhibited from further preaching, and although he had gained some sympathy among his congregation, he removed from Cambridge.[7] The letter of inhibition was personally delivered and read by Richard Bancroft, then Bishop's chancellor, later Archbishop of Canterbury.

During his time in Cambridge he had met a minister of like mind, Robert Harrison, who was 'Maister of the Hospitall' (that is, Headmaster of the Grammar School) at Norwich. Browne removed to Norwich and lodged with Harrison after leaving Cambridge; it is possible that on the way he paid a short visit to a Puritan congregation at Bury St Edmunds. At Norwich for a time Browne became, like Harrison, a schoolmaster, and complaint was made in 1580 to Grindal, who was now Archbishop of Canterbury, by the 'Lordes of the Counsaile' that a company of 'lewde Scholemasters' was corrupting the minds of the children in East Anglia. It was during this period that Browne came to the conclusion that the only way of true Reformation must be by outward separation from the Church; he became, that is, a religious revolutionary, or separatist. In 1581 he paid another visit to Bury St Edmunds, and the Bishop of Norwich (Dr Freke) made complaint to Lord Burghley in a letter which mentioned as the salient point in Browne's character 'his arrogant spirit of reproving'. Burghley, who was a distant kinsman of Browne, wrote back indicating his opinion that Browne should be 'charitably conferred with and reformed', and this—though no doubt the Bishop of Norwich reckoned it easier to hold this view in London than in Norwich—saved Browne from immediate arrest. But Browne left Norfolk and went to London, where almost at once he was imprisoned for nonconformity. When this short term of imprisonment was over, he intended to return to Norwich, but was unwise enough to call again at Bury, and was there apprehended by order of the now impatient Freke. Freke wrote to Burghley that Browne was incorrigible, and Burghley seems for a time to have washed his hands of him, for in August 1581 he was again behind bars in London.

The Brownists—for such was the name that his followers were soon given by their detractors—began to feel that England was no place for them. Some thought to join the Presbyterians in Scotland, who were now in the third decade of John Knox's Reformation. But at the turn of the year 1581/2 Browne decided to go to Holland. The historic cause of this inspiration was the presence of a circle of Dutch merchants in Norwich, who visited that city regularly in the way of trade, and who heard Browne with more sympathy than the English found it in their hearts to give him. To Middelburg, then, Browne went, and there he remained about eighteen months. He found there a Puritan company led by ex-Professor Cartwright, and at first joined himself to them. But he soon formed a congregation of his own, finding it difficult to remain subordinate for long even to such a leader as Cartwright. At Middelburg he wrote his three famous tracts, *A Treatise of Reformation without Tarrying for Anie*, *A Treatise Vpon the 23 of Matthew*, and *A Booke which Sheweth the Life and Manners of all True Christians*.

Despite the presence of a congregation whose way of life he might have been expected to find sympathetic, Browne's stay in Middelburg was uneasy. Upon the situation there his own comment is illuminating: 'Instead of one Pope there, I found a thousand.' Returning to England he probably spent a short time at Stamford, and he may have made another short journey abroad. In 1585 he was certainly charged before Archbishop Whitgift as being the author of an anonymous pamphlet, *An Answer to Master Cartwright his Letter*; not that Whitgift would be thought eager to defend Cartwright, but rather that the matter of Browne's answer, if it was his, was deemed seditious. Browne signed a recantation, and was (about 1586) appointed master of St Olave's School, Southwark. The appointment was a gesture indicative of the renewed favour of Burghley, and despite Browne's frequent preaching in Dissenting conventicles, which were becoming increasingly suspect, Burghley supported him in a controversy with Howland, bishop of Peterborough, in 1589. At last in 1591 Browne took deacon's and priest's orders, and from that year until 1631 he was rector of Achurch, Northamptonshire. But during ten years of that period (1617–27) he was suspended, and lived at a nearby village, preaching to a small Dissenting congregation. In 1632, well beyond the age of eighty, he was imprisoned for the thirty-second and last time, and deprived of his living, and he died in October 1633.

There, embodied in a single person, is sixteenth-century English Dissent. During all his long life there can hardly have been a month during which Browne was not on terms of acrid controversy with some religious person or system. At some time or other he succeeded in disagreeing with representatives of every current religious view.

And yet there is at the centre of his convictions, from which he never allowed himself to be diverted, one positive proposition of the utmost importance. It is not new, but it is here put with unexampled force, and it is that only proved Christians can constitute a Church. Christians alone! That is where the controversy of historic English Dissent always begins. It is but a new knock on the old kaleidoscope. Holiness is inseparable from the gathered and covenanted Church; and Christians must be separated uncompromisingly from 'the world'. The highest possible voltage of corporate and personal holiness must be looked for in the company of believers: and this makes necessary a measure of Dissent from everything that is of secular authority, whether it be secular magistrates who attempt to exert authority in the Church, or secular-minded bishops who impose canon law on it.

Now of course the great question, how we are to judge which of our neighbours is and which is not a 'true believer', is a question requiring either an answer, or a direct and reasoned refusal to answer, from any church order. It is the mark of historic Dissent that while its feelings on the matter were always well marked and strongly worded, their doctrines on it have always been the most indecisive of all. Cartwright, at any rate, thought one thing; Henry Barrowe (of whom more in a moment) thought another; and Browne agreed with neither.

In Browne's view it was impossible for any company of Christians to be in any sense legalistically constituted. Of the popish churches (in which he would include virtually all Anglicans) he wrote in *The Life and Manners*:

How do they establish their false church and government? They are first under one chief antichrist, the Pope, or under other antichrists which resemble him, or spring up of him, and receive their image and marks.... They make their supper of a communion, a pledge and seal of their wretched confusions.

This he contrasts with that 'Communion of Graces', which is the true Church:

a mutual using of friendship and callings, to pleasure and be pleasured in all Christian charity. It is builded first by communion of the graces and offices in the Head of the church, which is Christ; secondly, by communion of the graces and offices in the body, which is the church of Christ. Thirdly, by using the Sacrament of the Lord's Supper, as a seal of this communion.[8]

That is good historic Dissenting sentiment. It is a man's right to have free and direct 'communion of the graces of Christ'; and this he has only in a church order which permits him 'communion of the graces' of his fellow men. The impediments to this free 'communion' are, first, an authoritarian church government, second, a legalistic church order, and third, a too casual reception into the Church of those whom the early Puritans roundly designate 'the ungodly'. These three stand or fall together; you cannot talk freely with one another in a company which may include, as it were, spies, philistines, and anarchists, neither can you form such a company of free-speaking friends at the direction of some bishop who lives a hundred miles away, or some secular patron who wants to find work for the fool of a neighbouring family. That is, as it were, what Browne was saying, if it be demythologized. And so far as he is concerned, the present ways of administering the Church cannot fall too soon. Once they are fallen he hopes for a large measure of co-operation and consultation between congregations in 'synods or meetings of sundry churches, which are when the weaker churches seek help of the stronger, for deciding or redressing of matters'.[9] At this point it is clear that Browne is much more than merely destructive of church order. A wild anarchistic Independency in which nobody takes any notice of his neighbour, though attributed to him by some, is the very reverse of his aim. He seeks the 'communion of graces' not only between members of a congregation but also between one congregation and its neighbours.

The place of this Dissenting ethos within the pattern of church order can best be illustrated by reference to the passage in St Matthew xviii where our Lord is reported as recommending a threefold order of church discipline. 'If your brother sins against you, go and tell him his fault, between you and him alone. If he listens to you, you have gained your brother. But if he does not listen, take one or two others along with you, that every word may be confirmed by the evidence of two or three witnesses. If he refuses to listen to them, tell it to the church; and if he refuses to listen even to the church, let him be to you as a Gentile and a tax-collector' (vv. 15–18). Whatever may be the answers to the exegetical problems presented by that text, we have there a very fair illustration of the Catholic tradition as it prevailed in Browne's time. Failing Christian forbearance and acceptance of private rebuke, let the Church admonish. Failing the good effect of the admonition, there is no more that the Church can do and the law must be left to take its course.

The medieval interpretation of that is familiar enough. Scandals, it was assumed, could not be prevented. At best, they should be privately settled; at second best, they should be settled by church courts; at worst, let the secular arm be invoked. In different ways, most comprehensive church orders presuppose a pattern of that kind— private discussion, church discipline, excommunication (which last is now normally interpreted as the permission for a membership to lapse).

But to Browne the emergence of scandals is in theory impossible, because the Church must in the first place take every possible precaution against the presence of 'sinners' in its ranks. Since on his theory this can only be achieved by a free church order that leaves the way open for a direct communication to the Church, on any given point, of the will of the Holy Ghost, it follows that Papacy and episcopacy are to him the very causes of the scandals that are manifest in the Church. Of any scandal he always says in effect, 'That would never have happened if you had not assented to Papacy and episcopacy'. On his view, authoritarian church orders are to be resisted because they make the Church safe for sinners.

Now this is, of course, a romantic notion. It bears no relation to human experience, to doctrine or to history. It is only by rejecting out of hand St Augustine's doctrine that the Church must need contain sinners and suffer impurities that Browne can begin on his work of 'purifying' the Church. The evidences from history that any attempt to 'purify' it beyond a certain point always comes to grief he would dismiss as medieval and therefore inadmissible. As for ordinary human experience, it is unregenerate and therefore of no consequence.

To be fair to Browne, it ought to be said that almost certainly he early gave up hope of being merely a reformer, and of making the Church of England a 'pure' church. He was by temperament and doctrine a revolutionary who sought no more than to prophecy from outside the Church, and to show a better way by the example of his small gathered congregations. If he has to be reckoned an eccentric, a 'fringe-man', whose doctrines, though practicable at the local level, could never be applied universally without either contradiction or serious modification from within, he is of those who are content to be so called. But historically his example proved to be the inspiration of a development that for a short while occupied a prominent place in English secular history, and which, culminating in the martyrdoms of 1593, did more than Browne himself could have hoped to do towards establishing Dissent as something more than a vexatious deviation.

3. *The Marprelate tracts and the Tyburn executions*

It is at this point that the movements of larger-scale European politics are forced on the notice of the historian of English Dissent. They are never very far from the edge of the picture, but we may say that when Mary I designated Philip of Spain the heir to the English throne she made sure of a continuing and fierce political Dissent in England of a kind which the Protestant religious Dissent might have expected to be favourable to its own aims.

As it turned out, this is by no means what happened. But in 1558 there was a very large and powerful body of opinion in England which looked with horror on the thought of a return to a Catholic throne. The body which took the opposite view was reduced, after 1558, to the status of a more or less underground movement, and Catholics were regarded as the arch-enemies of English security and English national interests. It is impossible, of course, to distinguish finally between those who hated the thought of Philip of Spain *qua* Roman Catholic, and those who feared him *qua* Spaniard; if it were possible so to distinguish, it would be less easy than it is to judge that English Protestantism in the Elizabethan age was very closely involved with English nationalism. Undoubtedly it was so: but what we must here notice with particular care is that it was a new kind of middle-of-the-road Protestantism, a Protestantism that favoured the Establishment, a Protestantism that dissented from Rome but not from the Queen and the Queen's church order, that was the backbone of the Elizabethan age. And to dissent from *that*—Protestantism as represented by the English queen and the English bishops—was to ask for trouble, whatever else you might favour or protest against.

England during the years 1558–88 became increasingly security-sensitive. The crisis came at the end of that generation. In Spain and England alike we have, in 1587–8, the strange spectacle of two dogmatic yet strategically cautious sovereigns being driven into decisive action by pressure of their courtiers' and generals' opinions. In our own country, Elizabeth signed the warrant for the execution of Catholic Mary of Scotland, and no action she ever took was taken with deeper misgiving. Partly in consequence, Philip in Spain capitulated to the ambitions of his naval commanders and ordered the dispatch of the Armada in a holy crusade against Britain, whose image in Philip's mind H. A. L. Fisher happily caught in the phrase 'that island of formidable heretics'.[10]

Once the decision had been taken, the Armada represented a gesture both against the Protestant errors of Britain symbolized in the persecution of Catholics and in the beheading of Mary of Scotland, and against the buccaneering imperialism of Sir Francis Drake. And once defeated, the Armada represented to Englishmen a contemptible foreign Catholic presumption. It is probably unwise to compare the atmosphere in 1588 with that of England in 1940, when another and more devastating invasion was in prospect. Yet there was something of the same sense of urgency in the manner in which the coast of southern Cumberland was suspected of being a landing-place for Catholic sympathizers. But the nineteen-forties provide no parallel to that spirit of Elizabethan Merrie-Englandism which produced, along with so much enterprise that we have been taught to regard as admirable, a somewhat school-prefect-like intolerance and contempt of dissents and eccentricities. People were beginning to adopt that frame of mind which would later use the word 'un-English' with a certain intonation to mean politically or racially or religiously nonconformist.

This has to be understood before we can explain the astonishing fact that in the prisons of London men lay awaiting death in 1593 some of whom, like Henry Barrowe and Thomas Greenwood, were obstinate in Protestant dissent from the Church of England, and others of whom, like Blessed Robert Southwell, were obstinate in Catholic dissent from it. Brownist pamphleteer and Catholic *beatus* were alike—and to the great embarrassment especially of Protestant historians of later days—in Dissent from the new Anglicanism.

That State violence was now added to State and Church censure was as much as anything due to the publication of a series of documents known as the Marprelate tracts, which appeared in 1589/90. Their anonymous author has defied modern historical detectives in their attempt to establish his identity for certain; he is usually thought to be John Penry, a young and undoubtedly fiery Welshman, but there are six others with a claim to this distinction, one of whom, Udall, we shall have to mention again in a moment.

William Pierce, of whom the reader should be warned that, though an able and laborious scholar, he is very

firmly disposed towards the Puritan side, describes the
writings of 'Martin Marprelate' as 'an interesting novelty
in English literature'.[11] It is no doubt his Puritan pre-
dilection that causes him to refer to the anti-Marprelate
tracts, commissioned by Richard Bancroft, as 'the foundation of the yellow press'. The truth is that it was the
Marprelates that form the new gesture in journalism. They
combine, in a manner which was never surpassed, these
four qualities—a passionate and patriotic devotion to a
religious cause, a true gift for vivid writing, a discon-
certingly extensive dossier of the private lives of their
subjects, and a fierce humour that makes play with ironies,
mock-debates, nonsense-words, and a kind of bilious
slapstick that makes better entertainment than argument.
In one sentence we have an echo of the authentic Puritan
dignified dogmatism, in the next, language that makes us
suspect that William Shakespeare must have had the
tracts in mind when he composed the nonsense-speeches
of his clowns. It is the first appearance in England of the
'Publish and be Damned' technique: a burning social and
religious conscience finding expression in unscrupulously
personal and particularized language handled by a born
columnist.

The primary target of Martin Marprelate is the bishops
—all bishops, and the principle of episcopacy in general,
and certain bishops in particular. Here the chief Reforming ingredients are patriotism and holiness: Marprelate presents himself as a patriot, a true lover of
England, who would purge the Church of its corruptions.
Here are the first words on the title-page of the first tract:

An Epistle to the Terrible Priests. To the right puissant and
terrible Priests, my clergy-masters of the Confocation-house,
whether Fickers-general, worshipful Metropolitans, or any other

of the Holy League of Subscription: this work I recommend to them with all my heart, with a desire to see them all so provided for one day, as I would wish, which I promise them shall not be at all to their hurt.[12]

On the uproar that followed the publication of the first tract, 'Martin' writes in the second (briefly known as the *Epitome*):

Martin Mar-Prelate, Gentleman, Primate and Metropolitan of all the Martins in England, to all clergy-masters wheresoever, saith as followeth: Why, my clergy-masters, is it even so with your Terribleness? May not a poor gentleman signify his good will unto you by a Letter, but presently you must put yourselves to the pains and charges, of calling four bishops together...and posting over city and country for poor Martin?

And of what style of modern journalism (indeed of what modern English institution, thus to be surprisingly ascribed to a branch of Dissent) is the reader reminded by this?

Who made the porter of his gate a dumb minister? Dumb John of London. [*sc.* John Aylmer, Bishop of London.] Who abuseth her majesty's subjects in urging them to subscribe contrary to law? John of London. Who Buseth the High Commission, in as much as any? John London (and Dr Stanhope too). Who bound an Essex minister in £200 to wear the surplice on Easter Day last? John London....Who is a carnal defender of the breach of the Sabbath in all places of his abode? John London....Who goeth to bowls on the Sabbath? John London. Dumb, duncical John of good London hath done all this.[13]

Here are two consecutive charges (the first two of thirty-seven) made in the third tract, mock-comically called *Certain Minerall and Metaphysicall Schoolpoints to be defended by the Reverend Bishops*...('minerall' is a malapropism for 'moral'):

1. That the Puritans may as well deny the Son of God to be... consubstantial with God the Father, as they may deny the superiority of archbishops and bishops to be lawful. The defendant in this point is Father John of Fulham in his preface before Bernardeus de Loques' Book of the Church, published in English.

2. That a L.B. [i.e. a Lord Bishop] may safely have two wives *in esse* at once. The defendant in this point is Father Marmaduke, Bishop of St David's, who hath two now living, the one Elizabeth Giggs, the other, Alice Prime, Proved against him in the High Commission.[14]

Not infrequently a wrong name or a misascribed reference provides work for the commentators; often the argument is faulty and the premisses are dubious. But never before, and surely hardly since, was so particularized and devastating a series of documents released in an English religious cause.

May it please your honourable worships to let worthy Martin understand why your Canterburyness and the rest of the Lord Bishops favour Papists and Recusants rather than Puritans.... Send Wigginton home to his charge again....Let the Templars have Master Travers their preacher restored again unto them.... Will you not send Master Wyburn to Northampton, that he may see some fruits of the seed he sowed there sixteen or eighteen years ago?...Briefly, may it please you, let the Gospel have a free course, and restore unto their former liberty in preaching all the preachers that you have put to silence.[15]

The author of the pamphlets exposes every case of (in his own eyes) unlawful inhibition and ecclesiastical jobbery that he knows of; and it adds up to a formidable campaign on the part of the bishops to root out Puritan Dissent. The constructive side of his argument is far less consistent than the destructive; but it evinces a typical Puritan–Calvinist view, a hatred of sabbath-breaking, a contempt for an unworthy ministry, a singular loathing of the bishops' demand that Bibles must always contain the Apocrypha (a collection of books always regarded as totally unworthy of Scripture by the Reformers), and a declared purpose to see all these abuses removed. 'I will place a Martin in every parish. In part of Suffolk and Essex I think I were best to have two in a parish.'

The publication of these tracts was, of course, a business that makes a story worthy of our best contemporary thriller-writers. Public printing-presses were already inaccessible to Dissenters. The first of the tracts was printed on a secret press at Moulsey, near Kingston upon Thames, whose vicar, John Udall (or 'Uvedale'), was suspected for this reason of being their author. The press moved to Fawsley House, Northamptonshire, for the publication of the *Epitome* (no. 2), and to White Friars, Coventry, to print the *Mineralls* and *Hay Any Worke for Cooper* (nos. 3 and 4). The last three, *Theses Martinianae, Martin Junior's Epilogue*, and *The Protestation*, come from the Priory, Wolston, 'the residence of Roger Wolston, Esq.', and when the press was finally discovered, it was at Manchester. The first is dated October 1558, the seventh, September 1589.

The first trial that followed the detection of the printers was that of Udall. This was first and last a security-trial, with a strange high-toned religious savour reminiscent of certain kinds of modern political trial. The avowed object of the prosecutors was to get Udall to admit that he had written a tract called *A Demonstration of Discipline* (1590). If he could be got to admit that he had also written the Marprelates, a matter that was brought up again at a second trial at Croydon, so much the better. The jury were instructed that not so much punishment as repentance was the judge's aim if the prisoner were found guilty; indeed, that it would be good for the prisoner's soul if he were found guilty.[16]

Udall loftily ignored all this. He firmly refused to sign a confession which was drawn up for him. But with typical Puritan rectitude and faithfulness to the letter, Udall wrote out himself a statement that although he was not the author

66

of *A Demonstration*, he could not disavow the sentiments it contained, and that he threw himself on the Queen's mercy.

This was enough for the judges, and he was committed to the Fleet, where Penry, Greenwood and Cartwright were already lying. The rest of the story is familiar. Three years the great company of Dissenting felons lay in that prison, until in 1593 they were taken out to be hanged at Tyburn.

And they were hanged for sedition. As Daniel Neal says of Udall's trial,

To prove the sedition, and bring it within the statute, the counsel insisted upon his threatening the bishops, who being the Queen's officers, it was construed as a threatening of the Queen herself. The prisoner desired liberty to explain the passage, and his counsel insisted, that an offence against the bishops was not sedition against the Queen but the judge gave it for law, that 'they who spake against the Queen's government in causes ecclesiastical, or her laws, proceedings and ecclesiastical officers, defamed the Queen herself'.[17]

Since the trials were for sedition, it was natural that the patriotic note should be sounded in the defences. As John Penry wrote in his own defence,

I never took myself for a rebuker, much less for a reformer of states and kingdoms; far was that from me; yet in the discharge of my conscience all the world must bear with me, if I prefer my testimony to the truth of Jesus Christ before the favour of any creature, An enemy to good order and policy either in this church or commonwealth was I never....If my death can procure any quietness to the church of God or the State, I shall rejoice.[18]

Udall went even farther in his final 'confession of faith':

I believe, and have often preached, that the church of England is a part of the true visible church, the word and sacraments being truly dispensed...and do still desire to be a preacher in the same church; therefore I utterly renounce the schism and separation of the Brownists.[19]

Penry, in *A Treatise wherein it is manifestly proved that the Reformation, and those that sincerely favour the same, are unjustly charged to be enemies unto her Majesty and the State*, near the beginning wrote,

As for attempting any undutiful or disloyal action in the promoting of the cause itself, we have been so far from being guilty... that one of our most shameless and most impudent slanderers was enforced to pass by us, and did suffer the venom of his lying and slanderous tongue to light upon our brethren in the kingdom of Scotland, which he would never have done if with any colour he could have fastened his slanderous untruths upon us the professors of his own country.[20]

These men, then, claimed to be the true patriots. And although much of the claim was forced from them by the charge of sedition, there remains justice in their implication that they mean no ill to the State, and are astonished to be found in company with those fifth-columnists, the Roman recusants. It is just because it was their conviction that the Church and the State must be separated that they were able to make this point strongly. Their argument against their prosecutors amounts here to this: 'You accuse us of treason; but that is the consequence of the error we insist on ascribing to you, namely your confusing what is of the State with what is of the Church. We seek to reform the Church: to the State, except in so far as it presumes to interfere with the Church, we wish no ill.'

The reform of the Church was a matter in which, as we have already implied, Dissenters disagreed among themselves in details. Udall was relatively conservative, believing in the government of the Church by ministers assisted by elders—that is, in Presbyterianism. Given this, and what he deemed a proper method of appointing ministers and elders, he allowed that 'the censures of the Church ought merely to concern the soul, and may not impeach any subject, much less any prince, in liberty of body, goods, dominion, or any earthly privilege'.[21] Cartwright and that Walter Travers whom Martin Marprelate wished restored to his ministry (he was a Fellow of Trinity College, Cambridge) devised a church system which they called the 'classis' system, and which was designed to replace the existing dioceses and parishes by a system of synods throughout the country, each responsible to a county-synod, and through the county to a national Assembly. The business of the local synod or 'classis' was principally to moderate in any situation where a church was looking for a pastor, and to see that worthy pastors alone were appointed to livings: to the county synods the special duty of almsgiving and relief of deprived ministers was allotted. This system was based on a similar pattern adopted by the Protestants in Holland. Cartwright and Travers favoured it, but Henry Barrow of Gray's Inn, who perished at Tyburn in 1593, dissented from that system as being too clericalized.[22] The theological system of Calvin was in general accepted by these Dissenters, but Barrow dissents from it at certain vital points, preferring a more liberal theology and church government, and in the matter of the Sacraments he is at odds with Penry.[23]

Indeed, the more assiduously one reads the enormous literature that was poured out in two or three years by these controversialists, the more one is driven to two conclusions. The first is that no two Dissenters thought exactly alike on all matters with which they were concerned: but the second is that a quite clear 'spirit of Dissent' emerges from the total sum of the pre-1593 documents. And that spirit is the old Reformed spirit—dissent against a State connection which smelt strongly of Rome, dissent against an unworthy priesthood that naturally came from this

State connection, and dissent against mental and spiritual bondage. In the constructive methods of reform, they all disagreed; but in these overarching ideas they concurred.

It was their concurrence in this Reformed view that gave them what unity they possessed. From that unity they derived at any rate strength to be obstinate under the duress which the State brought to bear. From that unity they gathered strength alike to face the wrath of Archbishop Whitgift, in whose name the treason-trials were conducted, and (what may have been much more difficult to face) the gentle reasoning of Lancelot Andrewes. For it is on record—as one of the sadder ironies of this chapter of history—that Udall was frequently visited by Andrewes, who was at the time Vicar of St Giles, Cripplegate, and who sought to persuade him to withdraw his reforming contentions.[24] There were two enigmatic men facing one another! The young Anglican priest, about 35, destined to turn down two bishoprics because a condition of his accepting them was an alienation of certain of their emoluments, and to accept a third which brought him much strife and controversy; destined to become the saint of the *Preces Privatae*, a true lover of the new English Church order; and the even younger Dissenter, perhaps about 28, stern, upright, humourless, scrupulous, bound for the traitor's gallows. Which of these had the more to learn when the day of reckoning came for him?

CHAPTER VI

COMING OF AGE, 1593–1660

1. *Curious doctrines at Cambridge*

It is difficult to estimate the effect which the executions of the Brownists had on public opinion in England. Different historians offer different views according to their predispositions. It is probably safe to say that after 1593 Dissent was firmly settled as an English institution, even if, paradoxically, it was after that date that the great exodus of Dissenters from England to the Continent really began. We may judge, anyhow, that the Queen and the Archbishop by no means carried public opinion with them when they devised these executions. The Queen's private mind, inscrutable on this as on all other of the momentous decisions which had to be taken in her reign, will never be known. What we do see is a settling into the texture of English religious life of a moderate Puritan opinion which turned out to wield an enormous power towards the shaping of the habits of the English Church in the following century.

If the Brownists tended, after 1593, to make their way to such continental cities—especially in Holland—as they expected would offer them better hospitality than Whitgift's England, and if they took with them their high views on ministerial holiness and congregational purity, there remained in this country many who devoted much energy to the forwarding of the third Puritan value—that of enlightenment. As might be expected, after 1593 the Puritan controversialists tended to argue theological rather than moral or political cases. This, after all, was a good deal safer.

The University of Cambridge, the home of Cartwright and of so much Dissenting thought, continued in subtler ways to trouble the ecclesiastical peace. In 1595 Nicholas Bownde (or Bound), Fellow of Peterhouse, published a treatise on the very Puritan theme *The Doctrine of the Sabbath*, which precipitated a dispute between the Puritan legalistic view of the Sabbath and the more liberal view of the High-churchmen. Bownde's book was called in and confiscated by Whitgift, but it was republished immediately after Whitgift's death (1606).

In the same year William Barret, Fellow of Gonville and Caius, preached a University sermon *ad clerum*, in which he vigorously attacked that high Calvinist doctrine of Predestination which was widely held even by those who were in no other way to be called Puritans. This was especially unpopular in Cambridge, and he was called on to preach a retractation in the same church before the University authorities. The good-humoured cynicism of this retractation gave greater offence than the original sermon. Whitgift, petitioned to examine and remonstrate with him, rebuked him in terms so strong that he left the University, fled to France, and turned Roman Catholic. This placed him outside the approval of Neal, who calls him 'a conceited youth, who did not treat his superiors with decency'.[1] That, of course, is what you get from Neal if you turn Papist. The controversy, in itself a small affair, is of interest in that it bound Puritan opinion for a short season to approve of Whitgift when he produced, through an Archbishop's Committee, a document Calvinistic enough to keep the Seventeenth Article safe.

Then in 1599 Hugh Broughton, Fellow of Christ's, in a pamphlet designed as an 'Explication' of the credal article 'He descended into Hell', propounded the view that in the context 'hell' means not 'eternal punishment' but, as the Greek *hades*, 'the world of the dead'. This—which fore-shows that classical, imaginative emphasis that distin-guished the Cambridge Platonists of a generation later, is another attack on John Calvin, whose doctrine that Christ experienced not only physical death but also divine wrath is clearly set out in his *Institutes*.[2] Here Puritan opinion, which criticized Broughton as closely as it had criticized Barret, was in the long run defeated: and rightly, in as much as Broughton was interpreting a Greek text and not a Hebrew or Aramaic-related one. The episode is signi-ficant in being perhaps the first considerable criticism offered to that literal bibliolatry which had been alike the habit of Puritan and High-churchman.

2. *The King James Bible*

It was at this academic level that discussion proceeded during the last ten years of the life of Elizabeth I. On the accession of King James I, events took a more dramatic turn. James I, whom Charles Williams in the Preface to his *James I* calls 'the most grotesque of our Kings', came from Scotland to find in England the Puritans ready to welcome him, and the Anglicans ready to suspect. But both sides had reckoned, in this anticipation, without the Jesuit and Presbyterian plots which had already vexed James in the north. James himself approached the English Church with a sense of relief and safety. Conspiracy, at any rate, was not to be expected from bishops. When the Hampton Court Conference was called, therefore, at the very beginning of his reign, it provided at its outset some surprises for both sides. When the matter of episcopacy in the Church of England was raised by this historic gathering of nine Anglican dignitaries and four Puritans, the King declared in an historic epigram his views on the matter: 'No bishop, no King.' Very little concession was offered to Puritan opinion in the matter of the Book of Common Prayer. But that which was inaugurated on 15 January 1604 (new style) sufficiently compensated Puritan opinion for much of which it was to be disappointed. It was on that day that Dr John Reynolds (or Rainolds), leader of the Puritan party, rose to put the historic question, 'May your Majesty be pleased that the Bible be new translated, such as are extant not answering the original'. Archbishop Bancroft broke in at once with the remark that 'if every man's humour might be followed, there would be no end of translating'. But Reynolds had the royal ear, for King James was himself highly critical of the existing translations, and was found to approve the project. The result of this, seven years later, was the publication of the King James, or Authorized, Version of Scripture.[3]

The Authorized Version is historically the meeting-point of Puritan and High Church devotion. History would indeed be almost too stark to bear or understand did it not provide these occasional compensations for its terrifying ironies. Here is Reynolds, a non-separatist Puritan of marked Calvinist sympathy, highly critical of the Elizabethan church order, destined with his colleagues to drink deep of the royal contempt, putting a motion which of all others was dear to the Puritan conscience: and there, at the head of the list of translators appointed to make a new version of the first thirteen books of the Old Testament, is the name of Lancelot Andrewes.

There is nothing gained now by insisting that the Authorized Version is Puritanism's gift to the English Church. In a narrow sense, no doubt it was: Reynolds wanted it, Bancroft did not want it. But it is the best gift to the English Church that the enlightening spirit of the Renaissance provided. Here is the official, indeed the royal, charter for vernacular Bibles, in a sentence from the Translators' Preface:

How shall men meditate in that, which they cannot understand? How shall they understand that which is kept close in an unknown tongue? Translation it is that openeth the window to let in the light; that breaketh the shell that we may eat the kernel; that putteth aside the curtain, that we may look into the most Holy place; that removeth the cover of the well, that we may come by the water.

It was the translators' purpose 'not to make a new Translation, nor yet to make of a bad one a good one; but to make a good one better, or out of many good ones, one principal good one'. They had, they claimed, avoided alike the 'scrupulosity of the Puritans' and the 'obscurity of the Papists'.

It is worth adding to these worthy opinions this comment further: that the very nature of this translation affords an illuminating illustration of what was now happening to English religious opinion. The Authorized Version has always been admitted to be a monument of English literature. There are many nowadays who, having rejected all Christian allegiance, are swift to confess their admiration for the Bible as literature; and even if at certain points it is an unsafe authority for modern syntax, as where we read 'Whom do men say that I, the Son of Man, am?' or 'I sanctify myself, that they also might be sanctified', it is idle to attempt to impugn the notion that this is great literature. But, as Professor C. S. Lewis once pointed out,[4] it is a very strange and special kind of literature. It is not written in what from any other source we infer to be seventeenth-century or Elizabethan English. Its rhythms could not be less like those of Sir Francis Bacon. This, as is obvious, is because it is a very faithful translation of Hebrew and Greek originals; it is the most literal translation that those scholars could compass; where they sought to 'improve' on earlier versions, the improvement was in the direction of closer literalness. Every word to which no word in the original corresponded was printed in italic. The translators avoided, they said, Puritan scrupulosity and Popish obscurity. But they achieved the most felicitous blend of Puritan precision with Catholic awe. This national monument is a symbol, as it is the only historic example, of the perfect blending of the tradition of orthodoxy with that of Dissent; and it was brought about by the sudden, unexpected nod of 'the most grotesque of English kings'.

That decided, the Hampton Court Conference turned to other business, and broadly speaking the Puritans lost every trick. In the end, after much debate about 'the purity of Christ's Church', during which Reynolds and his friends brought up again the familiar objections to the wearing of surplices, the use of the ring in marriage, and the churching of women, together with certain disciplinary suggestions such as a three-weekly prayer-meeting for all clergy, the King turned on Reynolds and said 'If this be all your party hath to say, I will make them conform at once themselves, or else I will harry them out of the land or else do worse'. Charles Williams observes of this: 'It was a great day's work for the future. Between them all they had promised the Authorized Version, and determined the inevitability of the Nonconforming Churches.'[5]

Williams is surely right. Even more than 1593, this settled Dissent into the English scene. The executions of Tyburn drove the dissidents from the country; the Hampton Court Conference drove the non-separatists very largely into a separatism that was to provide a welcome for the returned exiles of 1640, and that was to breed an Oliver Cromwell.

3. *The continental separatists and the first Baptists*

Leyden, Middelburg and Amsterdam had cheerfully received the exiled Brownists during the last years of Elizabeth's reign, and it was there that they began to learn the historical lessons of Independency. Their leading teacher was Henry Ainsworth (1570–1622), sometime Fellow of St John's, Cambridge, who became minister to the exiles in Amsterdam in 1596 and wrote, or partly wrote, the *Confession of Faith of the People called Brownists* (1596). Dissent in England from 1593 to 1640 was very largely Presbyterian, following Calvin through Cartwright and Udall. The continental form of exiled English Dissent tended to be Brownist and Congregational; but there are three major movements of religious history that come from this continental exile. One of these is that re-injection of Independency into English Dissent in 1640, and with that we shall deal a little later on. The two others are the rise of the Baptist movement and the emigration of the second-generation Brownists to the New World.

Anabaptism, we recall, included in its vigorous statement of the Reformed claim a doctrine that baptism must be administered only to those who were of an age to make personal responsible assent to the Sacrament by taking for themselves the vows associated with it. This aspect of the Reformed claim does not seem to have found a place in the earlier English Dissenting claim, but it was inevitable that certain consciences should be exercised by it. The religious denomination now known as 'General Baptist' or, more simply, 'Baptist' traces its foundation to John Smyth

77

(sometimes Smith), who was a Fellow of Christ's College, Cambridge, and an Anglican clergyman. He fairly soon became a separatist, and gathered a congregation at Lincoln (1603–5). Later he emigrated with his people to Amsterdam, and there began to preach and put into effect the doctrine of adult baptism. He first baptized himself (from which action he was known to some as the 'Se-baptist'), and then baptized his congregation, calling them 'The Brethren of the Separation of the Second English Church at Amsterdam'. Thereafter membership of this congregation was conditional on the believer's undergoing adult baptism. Naturally, Smyth found that the continental Mennonites, or latter-day Anabaptists, were much in sympathy with his proceedings. He died in 1612, but members of his congregation, on returning in that year to London, established there the first Baptist church at Pinners Hall, where one of their number, Thomas Helwys (d. c. 1616), became the first minister.

Thereafter the Baptists became an established and influential body among English Dissenters. Their sympathies were invariably with the left wing of Dissent, and their church polity was, and has remained, identical with that of the Independents. This is not the place to discuss the theological merits of the view of Baptism which distinguishes the Baptist churches. It suffices here to observe that being thus distinguished from other Christians on a sacramental plane, whereas the divisions between the Christian denominations are more usually in the plane of ecclesiastical polity, the Baptists have by this special separatism become a Christian company of enormous influence and importance. Their world communion today numbers between thirteen and fourteen million. At the time of their beginning, the Baptists helped to establish certain habits and views of church life not only among themselves but also among those Independents who were their nearest neighbours and from whom they at first separated. We owe the persistence of the typically Brownist church temperament—a deep suspicion of church liturgies, ceremonies, and authorities, at least as much to the Baptists as to the Dutch Brownists, and this for two reasons: first, that the Baptists established their post-exilic churches in England rather earlier than the Independents established theirs, and were unwilling to assimilate them to that Presbyterianism which was the English Puritan habit at the time; and second because, being Baptists, and therefore in an additional sense Dissenters, they pursued their separatism with the greater zeal, and formed their habits with the greater assiduity.

4. *The Pilgrim Fathers*

The Brownists who remained in Holland formed themselves, as the second decade of the seventeenth century unfolded itself, into settled companies of earnest Christian believers. The people who composed these assemblies were on the whole people of responsible, educated and adventurous spirit. They were the new *bourgeois* who alike in England and in Holland—two cultures which had almost everything in common at that date—were forming a new national spirit and a new national economy. These were the people who were in the end responsible for a new attitude towards 'trade', who were beginning to make the career of a merchant respectable and respected. Here one found that 'independence of spirit' which reacted strongly against authoritarianism, and which welcomed that modified Brownism which was exemplified in such a leader as Pastor John Robinson of Leyden.

Robinson (d. 1625) is the most eminent, and seems to have been the best loved, of the exiled Independent religious leaders. Like so many Puritan notables, he held a Cambridge fellowship (at Christ's), and a curacy at Norwich (St Andrew's). Refusing to subscribe the Articles of Religion, he was in the usual way suspended from preaching. It was he who with William Brewster (d. 1644), the postmaster at Scrooby, Lincs, organized the major emigration of Independents to Leyden, and for some twenty years he remained their minister in that place. When the emigration to the New World was planned, it was Brewster who was appointed to lead the expedition, and Brewster who exercised the first ministry to the emigrants when they landed on the other side.

The *Mayflower's* historic voyage across the Atlantic in 1620, which has kindled the imaginations of so many, was a judicious blend of business and religion, in true Puritan fashion. On the one hand, the high aim of the emigrants was to found a new colony which should in very truth be a theocracy. That 'pure church' which had found a chilly welcome in England, and whose sojourn in Holland had been made uneasy by much internal dissension and much difficulty in adjusting new ideas to obstinate conservative natural habits, would, they reckoned, have room to breathe and grow in the new country of America. There was a blessed land where there were no bishops, and where there were not even any crusty deacons and men of old-fashioned mental make-up. There a hand-picked congregation from the saints of Leyden, free of everything that the Old World had put in their way, could make a new beginning in the name of the Lord.

But there also they could make a living. If ever there was a blend of the romance of travel and the down-to-earth

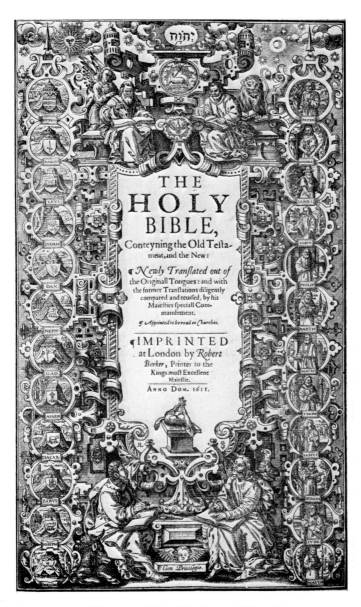

יהוה

THE
HOLY
BIBLE,

Conteyning the Old Testa-
ment, and the New:

¶ *Newly Translated out of*
the Originall Tongues: and with
the former Translations diligently
compared and reuised, by his
Maiesties speciall Com-
mandement.

¶ *Appointed to be read in Churches.*

¶IMPRINTED
at London by *Robert*
Barker, Printer to the
Kings most Excellent
Maiestie.

ANNO DOM. 1611.

Cum Priuilegio.

RVBEN · SIMEON · LEVI · IVDAH · DAN · NEPH · GAD · ASHER · ISACAR · ZABVL · IOSEPH

PETER · ANDRE · IAMES · IOHN · PHILIP · BARTH · MATH · THOM · IAMES · SIMON · IVDE · MATH

5 Title-page of the King James Bible, 1611

6   The exterior of Pinners Hall, 1815

business enterprise of the New Age, it was in this project to remove to the New World. It was remarked quite properly, apropos of the equally romantic and equally commercial (but less religious and less successful) *Mayflower* voyage of 1954, by the editor of a religious journal that nobody need really be greatly shocked by the business-note that was being sounded in the new venture, for that business-note was quite surely to be heard in the old one.[6]

It might fairly be said that the expedition lacked the organizing genius of a Drake, and that in the well-known story of the incredible hardships and horrors of the voyage, not to mention the first years of settlement, there is more than a hint of that inefficiency to which religious persons who involve themselves in secular enterprises feel themselves entitled. It was a badly organized and ill-equipped affair, but the crusading zeal and the commercial tenacity of the Englishmen who set out from Amsterdam, and of those others who joined them at Southampton, carried them, at considerable cost, through to their goal.

That meant that, once the Indians who inhabited the neighbourhood of Massachusetts Bay were driven out with that summary promptness which goes with no-non-sense business-minded Puritanism, small colonies with nostalgic English names like Boston and Plymouth began to grow. At this point, since this is not a history of world-Congregationalism, we must leave the story, making only one comment. That is that if you really want to see the full flower of the Puritan conceptual mind, the post-renaissance reverence for learning, the English-reformed insistence that the Word is at the centre of religion, you should go to New England.

The native religion of New England (not of Massachusetts, but of Boston) is Congregationalism on the

Leyden–Brownist pattern. The fact that nobody in the world was ever more strictly conformist in temperament than your New Englander of forty or fifty years ago is not a contradiction but an illumination of this. The difference between New England Congregationalism and Old-England Congregationalism is simply this—that in New England it was not a Dissent. What began, and continues, as a Dissent in England began in America as an orthodoxy: and if there was very little credal orthodoxy about it, it was a very formidable moral orthodoxy. The whole American constitution and way of life is ultimately founded on an orthodoxy that had been a Dissent in the countries it came from: that is the first and last of American religious and political history. The fact that America never tolerated a State Church meant that the idea of orthodoxy had at once to be transferred to morals and politics. A history of American Dissent would be a psychological and political story rather than a religious one.

But there at the heart of New England you can read in the inscription on the gate of Harvard University that that institution was founded in 1636 as a gesture expressing the great concern of the immigrants that the next generation should have a learned ministry. To this day the chief sacrament to the native religious mind of Boston is preaching; and the backbone of Protestant consciousness in New England is an orthodox Brownism whose ceremonies are grounded in the secular imagination, the social exactions, not in religious symbolism.

That, however, is by the way. John Robinson was left behind, and having parted at Southampton from his congregation, returned to his church at Leyden and died there within five years. Robinson was a convinced Independent in matters of church government; he had no use for the clericalism of English Presbyterian Dissent; he wrote much against the use of liturgies and ceremonies in church, expounding in pure form the doctrine that ceremony in religious observance is of the Old Covenant that has now gone, and that the believers of the new age should grow out of such childish things.[7] He was of those who preferred not to be known as 'Brownist', holding that they were no sect, but a company of the true Church. He was a gentle and godly example of the 'New Age' mind, and no more fitting person could have been chosen to inspire and exhort the men who took their families to New England in the New World. The most famous of his sentences, from his parting sermon to them at Southampton, 'The Lord hath let more light and truth to break forth out of his holy Word', fitly expressed this latest adventure of Lollardy which was to found the most prosperous, contradictory, energetic, confused, vivacious and hospitable nation of the modern world.

5. *The return of the exiles and the Westminster Assembly*
Much had been happening in England during the time when the extreme Dissenters were on the Continent, and to that we shall have to return. But the story of Brownist Dissent has its natural continuation in the behaviour of the returned exiles during the historic controversies of the years of the Long Parliament. Indeed, we reach a climax here, in that we come at last to the occasion on which the word 'Dissent' in the religious sense was coined.

During the reign of King James I of England, the Anglicans were, broadly speaking, in the ascendant. During that of his successor, the much less Puritan-tempered Charles Stuart, the situation suffered a dramatic reverse with the rise of Cromwell. To omit here that story to which we shall have to make later reference, the situation in the year 1640, in which the Long Parliament opened, was that England was broadly divided between the High Church Royalists, and the Puritan Roundheads. What matters at the moment is to note that these Puritans were Presbyterians. That is, they represented a body of opinion with which in the earlier generations many ministers of the Church of England had openly professed sympathy, and with which the Brownists of the exile were in controversy. You have, in 1640, a Dissent in England against Elizabethan Anglicanism promoted by a party from which the more extreme Brownists dissented with almost as much passion as either felt against the Anglicans.

When this Dissent became for a short season the orthodoxy of England, and the Royalist sympathizers were beginning to take thought for their very lives, their Parliament ordained that an Assembly of Divines should be convened at Westminster to formulate a church order for the new Church of England. It was (recall Petrie) in nobody's mind that England should have a tolerated Dissent. It was in the mind of the party in power that the Church of England should be Presbyterian: that is, that it should be ruled not through bishops but through presbyters and synods of presbyters. In more familiar language, this meant that the ministry must have sole control of the Church, without any interference from the State; and that there must be no official connexion with the State in any of its appointed officers.

Along these lines the Westminster Assembly sought to establish the new church order; and indeed in its Confession of 1645 and the accompanying Directory of Worship they did so establish it. But from the beginning it was clear that this would be a majority decision, not a unanimous one: and for certain very curious historical reasons the Presbyterian way never, even during the eclipse of Anglicanism, became the accepted English church order.

The Westminster Assembly was convened by an Act of Parliament dated 12 June 1643. The question whether it was to be an independent and self-governing Assembly of the Church, or whether it was in the last resort an advisory body to Parliament on church affairs was at once seen to be of crucial importance. Parliament had accepted, on 17 August 1643, the 'Solemn League and Covenant' with the Scottish Kirk, and directed that the Assembly should accept it, which it did on 25 September of the same year. This indicated a clear direction towards the principle that in the last resort Parliament was the source of church order, because that principle was accepted in the Covenant. Many dissented from it, and some, though continuing to hold their places in the Assembly, were never convinced of it. The Assembly was originally composed of 151 members, thirty of whom were 'commoners', or what are now called 'laymen', the rest, 'divines'. The parties represented are usually categorized as Episcopal, Erastian, Presbyterian and Dissenting. The 'Episcopals' were those who looked for a modified episcopacy in the reformed Church of England; the 'Erastians' those who were persuaded that the supreme rule of the State must not be upset, whatever reforms in church order were undertaken; the Presbyterians were in a large and absolute majority, and the Dissenters known to be in formal and decisive dissent from Presbyterianism numbered seven. It is five of these seven, who took a prominent part in the debates, who are called the 'Dissenting Brethren'. The Episcopals of Royalist sympathy were early forbidden by the King to

attend the Assembly, and the Erastians found the proceedings so little to their taste that they disappeared fairly
soon from its deliberations.

The details of the proceedings of this Assembly, which
continued through 1163 sessions from 1643 to the middle
of 1648, and survived a little longer as a body for the
examination of clergy, must not detain us here.[8] The
Dissent which arose in it was to be foreseen from its
beginning. At an early stage it was so marked that the
Assembly invited the 'Dissenting Brethren' to state their
case in a considered report. This report bears the title
*An Apologeticall Narration, Humbly Submitted to the
Honourable Houses of Parliament, by Tho. Goodwin,
Philip Nye, Sidrach Simpson, Jer. Burroughs, William
Bridge.* It is dated 1643.[9]

'The Dissenting Brethren', says S. W. Carruthers,[10]
'had a reputation beyond the Assembly for intractability.'
The context of this reputation is well illustrated in the
opening paragraph of their report.

The most, if not all of us, had ten years since (some more, some
less) several settled stations in the Ministry, in places of public
use in the Church, not unknown to many of your selves; but the
sinful evil of those corruptions in the public worship and government of this Church, which all do now so generally acknowledge
and decry, took hold upon our consciences long before some
others of our brethren.[11]

These men had all ministered on the Continent, and
returned to England during the preceding decade to take
charge of parish churches. The situation prevailing in the
country was one which understandably horrified them.
Anti-Puritan feeling in the reigns both of James I and
Charles I found certain unsavoury expressions. The somewhat preposterous impositions associated with the 'Book
of Sports', a declaration defining recreations permissible

on the Sabbath drawn up by Bishop Thomas Moreton of Lichfield in 1618 and required to be read weekly in the churches, was an example of the triviality of these proceedings. It was reissued in 1633, and ministers of Puritan mind who refused to read it were punished by fine or ejectment from their livings. The ferocious penalties demanded of William Prynne, barrister of Lincoln's Inn, who was tried for treason on the evidence of his anti-theatrical pamphlet *Histriomastix*, of John Bastwick, physician, for his book *Flagellum Pontificis*, and of Henry Burton, Rector of St Matthew's, Friday Street, for his 'seditious' preaching, all of which were exacted in the year 1633/4, indicated with what indignation the authorities regarded Puritanism.

But the very ferocity and ingenuity of these invasions of Puritan liberty both exacerbated Puritan opinion and indicated that that opinion was gaining ground. What the Dissenters maintained was, first, that this kind of disorder was not sufficiently provided against in the Presbyterian *ethos* governing the Assembly, and second that the uncompromising Puritan opinion they represented had a great weight of physical authority behind it in Cromwell and the army.

The *Apologeticall Narration* is entirely concerned with arguments against Presbyterianism on the assumption that only their Independent Church order will make England safe for Christianity.

When it pleased God to bring us his poor *Exiles* back again in these revolutions of the times...we found...our opinions and ways environed about with a cloud of mistakes and misapprehensions, and our persons with reproaches. Besides other calumnies, as of *schism* &c, ...that proud and insolent title of *Independency* was affixed to us, as our claim; the very sound of which conveys to all men's apprehensions the challenge of an exemption of all Churches from all subjection and dependance, or rather a trumpet of defiance against what ever *Power*, *Spiritual* or *Civil*, which we do abhor and detest: Or else the odious name of *Brownism*...must needs be owned by us....We believe the truth to lie and consist in a *middle way* betwixt that which is falsely charged on us, *Brownism;* and that which is the contention of these times, the *authoritative Presbyterial Government* in all the subordinations and proceedings of it.[12]

It is clear from the the the reply of the Presbyterians[13] that the Dissenters were too ready to suspect a tyrannical clericalism in the Presbyterian design for the Church. But the case they present in their document is a clearer case for a Reformed Church than that which the Presbyterians were able to present. This was natural. The Presbyterians had just emerged from a long period of subjection: they had power, but the power they had was associated with State power. The Long Parliament was Presbyterian in *ethos*, and not all of them, not even most of them, thought that a close relation with the State was prejudicial to good order in the Church. The Dissenters, on the other hand, were newly back in England after developing their church order in a climate much more favourable than that of England. Though they repudiate the name of Browne and dislike being called Independents, they retain more of Browne's spirit than the Presbyterians.

But their repudiation of 'Brownist' and 'Independent' is significant in this: that they are equally anxious not to be thought of as anarchists, and not to be thought of as teaching that within the Church there should be no authority and no communication between local bodies. This was of some importance because the signs that Puritanism was to develop a 'lunatic fringe' were already quite unmistakable. The Dissenters' contention was no more or less than this: that the Church of England must be rid of priestcraft. The old distinction between the special graces of the ordained priest and the 'laity' were of the 'Old Covenant' and had to go. Presbyterianism was taking insufficient steps to see that it did go. Dissenters preferred to refer to elders—in the end they distinguished 'teaching elders' and 'ruling elders', their 'pastors' being those who taught and ruled, their 'ruling elders' being those who 'ruled' without holding teaching office.[14] It is characteristic of this stream of Dissent ultimately to regard the ministry as part of an eldership, of which they say 'Where there is but one elder in a church, there cannot be an *eldership* or *presbytery*, as there cannot be a senate where there is but one senator',[15] implying that a sufficient ministry is not provided by a single pastor 'ruling' alone. Presbyterianism implies that a 'presbytery', the ruling instrument of the Church, is confined to ordained ministers.

On other disciplinary matters the Dissenters were at pains to show that their own system, less legal, more 'free' than the Presbyterian, was not, as their detractors thought, an invitation to bad doctrine and ecclesiastical anarchy. They contended that it had worked very well in Holland. Where a matter of discipline had to be dealt with, it was sufficient to provide that a local church, gathered with its elders, could determine its solution—with help, if that were required, from the members of neighbouring churches.[16] It was unnecessary always to insist that the ordained ministry was the only instrument of discipline.

It was in the course of this same report, the *Apologeticall Narration*, that the word 'Congregational', as it were accidentally, first found its present denominational significance. Here, at least, was a word more positive than 'Dissenting', more suggestive of good order than 'Inde-

pendent', and less tarnished with local associations than
'Brownist'. This has become the recognized designation
for those who at present continue in the tradition of that
Dissent which was there formulated.

6. *Cromwell and the Commonwealth*

Dissent in 1644 drew much of its boldness, and of what
is usually called by historians its 'disproportionate' influence, from the knowledge that Cromwell was behind it.
Here again we must touch but lightly on the historical
details of a figure who has been well served by biographers
and scholars.[17] In Cromwell we have, to put it briefly, the
staggering sight of an English Dissenter who becomes the
most notorious of English regicides. Cromwell was born
the heir of an aristocratic Puritan tradition. Hinchinbrooke
House, bought with money gained from the dissolution
of the monasteries, was the home of his father, Sir Oliver
Cromwell, who sold it to the Montagu family which still
reigns there. Cromwell's heritage was pure English
Protestantism; his temperament was, as near as makes no
matter, pure Separatist. One has only to look at the celebrated picture of him to feel that if there was one man
around whom the whole of English religious and political
Dissent could gather in all its fierceness, it was the possessor
of so broad a brow and, at the same time, so prominent
a jaw.

In 1640, when the curtain went up on the Great Rebellion, Cromwell was forty-one. The dates fitted exactly. At
a time when most men are able to see the shape of their
destinies and to match their powers to them, Cromwell
found his hour.

Under Charles I there was much to dissent from, whatever your religious views might be. Raised in the eyes of

some to the status of martyr by the act of Cromwell, Charles may take comfort in the traditional dissociation of martyrdom from personal merit. In the second year of his reign his forced loans to raise money for foreign enterprises provoked protest among fifteen of his peers. In 1628 the Petition of Right was presented to him by Parliament, with its implied accusation of tyrannical and unconstitutional practice on the King's part. In 1629 the House refused to rise at the royal bidding, and from 1629 to 1640 there was no Parliament. Charles's loyalty to the Duke of Buckingham, whom Parliament to a man distrusted, and to William Laud, archbishop of Canterbury, whose repressive policies can be either described in Fisher's ironic words as the direct cause of the foundation of New England and of the fall of Charles I,[18] or more directly as plain ecclesiastical despotism—these loyalties, agreeable and even admirable as private virtues, served Charles ill when it came to politics.

The situation was already explosive at the close of the 1629 Parliament: ten years later Charles's action in attempting to force the Book of Common Prayer on the heirs of John Knox in Scotland precipitated an armed rising. With this rising in Scotland, Cromwell threw in his lot, and so began the Great Rebellion.

From that moment, parliamentary meant Puritan and Royalist meant Anglican. It need not have been so. Dissent against Charles had an excellent leader in Thomas Wentworth, later Earl of Strafford. Wentworth was a signatory to the Petition of Right, and was implacably opposed to royal dictatorship; but he was equally implacable in his enforcement of High Church principles, so far as he was able, on the nation. But during the sixteen-thirties a long procession of yeomen and landowners of the kind who were born willing to serve the King turned towards the parliamentary cause, and when Cromwell came to found his New Model Army he found not only willing recruits but as much money as he needed.

And so the Rebellion became the Civil War, and the Royalist cause sank farther and farther into despair, until on 30 January 1649 all was over. The genius behind it all, the focal point of the rebellion, was a man whose guiding principle was the new Protestantism in a fiercely concentrated form. Debating with the army leaders at the famous colloquies of 1647, Cromwell called for and expected a biblical exposition and prayer at the opening of every session, a reference to the Scriptures at the making of every point. His campaign was conducted on the same principles that governed the deliberations of the Westminster Assembly a mile or two away. And when it came to his attitude to personal power, he agonized over his Bible to find where the right path lay. Here was the heir of Puritanism, of State-hating Puritanism, with the whole of the State power in his hands, and with men clamouring to make him king. He had the power to make the Church of England into a fellowship of Congregational churches. He had the power to kill or to let live, the power to save or to destroy. His arch-enemy had believed in the divine right of kings; he wrestled with a divine Providence that nearly broke him. The author of the Drogheda massacre, on which Dr Robert Paul pertinently comments that, like Hiroshima in 1945, there is a case for saying that it 'shortened the war',[19] was the man who could plead with the Scottish Covenanters 'in the bowels of Christ' to think it possible that they were mistaken.

Human character is always contradictory. Any man's personal estimate of Cromwell will be guided by his views on the principles for which Cromwell stood, and by the relative emphasis he gives to his ruthlessness, which another man will call his courage, and to his religion, which another will call his neurotic bigotry. We need go no farther here than simply to state that it was Cromwell who brought Dissent to its terrible triumph.

If one thing was certain about the Long Parliament it was that it would decisively establish the limitations of monarchy in England. History brought up behind the Long Parliament—whose treatment of Charles I returned to him in tenfold measure the insults and sorrows that he had laid upon Parliament—a weight of public opinion that stabilized its contentions into principles. It is worth remarking here that if we are able to rejoice today in a monarchy which has for over a century held the esteem of the people, and for fifty years its affection as well, that is to a very large extent a debt owed by modern Englishmen to the English Dissenters. That affection which now adorns the constitutional monarchy, though it took many generations to grow, could not have been brought into English life without the harsh history of 1640–60. During those years a monarchical principle was established swiftly where, had abated harshness protracted the process, the monarchy might have died at the hands of benevolent republicans. In the short space of thirty years, see how history lurches from this side to that: a weak and amiable king, seeking to be personal friends with everybody and turning tyrant; a rebellion under arms; the king murdered and a commonwealth established; the commonwealth dying for lack of a leader; and the restoration of the monarchy. That Restoration gave all the signs of reviving everything that had been grievous in the tyranny of the previous generation. Church Dissent was to suffer much

more yet; but just because a generation is less than a life-
time, and grandfathers' memories can be active, the
country was spared a repetition of 1649 in 1689. In some
ways the Restoration put the clock back; social historians
are especially conscious of these. But so far as the
monarchy specifically is concerned, the contribution of
English Dissent is as distinguished as it is paradoxical.

7. *Sects and excesses*

But what in Cromwell was raised to so prodigious a
temperature of religion and social conscience, in some
others unrestrained by reason and the mundane necessities
of statesmanship took less admirable forms. The ancient
superstition that the Puritans were fanatically opposed to
the artist's life and activity is given most of its colour by
the vandalisms of those members of Cromwell's army over
whom even the Lord Protector could not exercise personal
control. (The truth about the Puritans and art, principally
music and poetry, is better stated by saying that they
disapproved, not of all art, but of the kind of art which was
especially encouraged under the Restoration. But that is
another story.)[20] It is hardly necessary here to urge that the
reader distinguish between the essential theology and
theory of statecraft that formed Cromwell's policy and the
specific acts of destruction perpetrated by his soldiers in
English cathedrals. Even where it can be shown that
Cromwell expressed insufficient disapproval of such proceedings, it need not be argued that the Dissenting mind
was, at this stage, inimical to art as such.

Cromwell's soldiers are mentioned here only as an
illustration of the perfectly familiar fact that significant
movements in religion and politics always have their
lunatic fringe of undisciplined and often greedy men. At

various levels the surge of English Dissent was accompanied by such manifestations, in some of which can be seen more cupidity, material or spiritual, than heroism, while in others a very lofty moral and spiritual tone is the rule.

Lollardy made certain local and popular appearances in the activities of parties like the Diggers and Levellers. These were primarily eccentric social movements. John Lilburne (d. 1657) became the centre in 1647 of the 'Levellers', a group who sought the dissolution of Parliament and a truly democratic rule for the country. Gerrard Winstanley about 1649 gathered round him a company, called the 'Diggers', who sought to propagate a communistic way of life, and, to that end, took possession of certain Crown properties in common land and proceeded to cultivate them with their spades. Legal proceedings soon disposed of them.

These somewhat anarchical and defiant political dissents were paralleled on the religious side by such groups as the Fifth Monarchy Men, who revived the old millenarianism by predicting the imminent end of this present world, to be followed by the total reign of Christ, which would last a thousand years. It is the 'Fifth Monarchy' because in the Book of Daniel ii. 40–4 that is the pattern laid down.

But the new axis of religious fanaticism which is observable in the days of the Commonwealth is Illuminism—the doctrine of the Inner Light. That is a development of extreme importance. The most extreme form of this doctrine is to be found in a sect known as the Ranters—a group who denied outright the authority of Scripture, Christ, the Creeds and the Ministry: that is, they denied every authority whatever except the individual conscience, and as a result felt entitled to break every commandment in the calendar when the Inner Light gave them leave. These are described by Knox as 'Waif and stray Anabaptists looking for light',[21] and that is what they were—heirs of Anabaptist emotion without any Anabaptist discipline. It was the infection of the Mennonite form of Anabaptism that inspired them, together with a touch of that 'Familism' which Henry Nicholas had founded on the Continent, in an attempt to subsume all theology and church order under the 'inner light' to be found within what he called the 'Family of Charity'.

8. *Quakers*

It was George Fox's misfortune that the Ranters were (understandably) thought to be associated with the Quakers. This was, in fact, nothing but a journalistic misapprehension. Fox (1624–91) was a different style of person altogether from these lesser eccentrics. He had, on his scale, something of Cromwell's agonized integration of theology and practice. The name 'Quaker' came from Fox's admonition to Parliament in 1650 to 'tremble before the Lord', and, secondarily, from the enthusiastic behaviour of his earliest followers. But Fox was no merely effervescent revivalist. He, the arch-apostle in England of the 'inner light', sought to found a company of people who, thus responsibly guided, should make manifest the Christian way in separation from the orthodox churches.

Fox was one of the first really responsible religious leaders to accept the notion of an established and continuing Dissent. It is clear that Cromwell and John Owen wanted the Church of England to be Congregational, and that the Divines wanted it Presbyterian, just as much as Laud wanted it High Church. Fox did not want the Church of England to be Quaker. He simply wanted it, in the old-

7   Oliver Cromwell

8   John Milton

fashioned sense, 'pure'. And to this end he published his
'Rule for the management of meetings' in 1668, and in
referring to his society as the 'Friends of the Truth' coined
the phrase, 'Society of Friends', by which the Quakers are
still known.

There was something in Fox that distinguished Quakerism from Diggerism. There was something here that caused
his followers to be numbered among the continuing Dissenters of history, and that made the Society of Friends the
choice and philanthropic and influential body that it is
today. This was, it must be supposed, his refusal entirely to
repudiate the doctrine of the Church. He had interests
that were not merely of the present moment on earth, nor
merely of eternity, but looked ahead into history. It was
for that reason that he set down his 'Rules'. Beyond this,
he brought out into the open, and laid public emphasis on,
a technique of pacifism and non-violence which still
distinguishes the Friends, and which in the days of the
Commonwealth was perhaps the most shocking and
provocative gesture he could have made.

For their illuminism, the Quakers were regarded as an
'enthusiastic' sect, and in the popular mind others of
enthusiastic tendencies were assimilated to them. The
unhappy James Nayler (d. 1660) is the most celebrated of
these. Nayler was indeed a member of Fox's circle, but
when in October 1656, after being arrested and imprisoned
at Exeter, he was found riding from Exeter to Bristol sur-
rounded by a group of followers who sought by gesture and
word to re-enact the Triumphal Entry into Jerusalem with
Nayler as the central figure, he had gone far beyond any
point where Fox could have sympathy with him. This
profane little pageant resulted in Nayler's arrest and in
ferocious punishment at the hands of the magistrates.

What the story of the early Quakers goes to show, how-ever, is that during the Commonwealth period the reigning religious party was as intolerant of Dissent as ever its own enemies had been. Knox's comment is trenchant, if slightly naughty:

In the last analysis, Puritan England was concerned not so much to exact punishment, as to make a gesture; the world must be assured that English religion had not gone into the melting-pot. Catholics were twitting Anglicans with the existence of Puritanism; Anglicans were twitting Puritans with the existence of Quakerism; Puritans were twitting Quakers with the existence of Naylerism. And Nayler must be the scapegoat. He suffered as the *reductio ad absurdum* of the Reformation experiment, with every man's hand against him.[22]

That comment, which Reformed sympathizers will not altogether approve, exposes the pattern of things before the age of tolerated Dissent. In that pattern, you are bound to have Dissent within Dissent, the leaders of each party hoping to dispose of those below him. It is useless to pretend that the reigning Puritans of the Commonwealth period believed in toleration.

At each stage we have a version of the same process. Each dissents from the next above him because he fears an invasion of those religious rights which he believes to be his own. The propagation of the idea of these rights is an approximate description of the 'Reformation experiment', though it might be as true to say that the experiment was always being tried somewhere by somebody. But it is not unjust to say that at this period Anglicans hated Roman discipline, Presbyterians Anglican discipline, Congrega-tionalists Presbyterian discipline, Quakers Puritan disci-pline, and (in a remote sense) Nayler Quaker discipline. It is only necessary to add that Fox brings a new dimension into the pattern, and causes the stick to bend in a new direction. For in a sense, in making the 'inner light' not merely an individual principle (which the Ranters and Nayler were content to do) but a principle of church order, Fox was saying to the left-wing Puritan Dissenters, 'This is really what you mean; this is your church order without its inconsistencies'. And so, just when Puritanism—under Cromwell, Puritan Congregationalism—was becoming a powerful organized State-involved church order, Fox with his 'inner light' pulled the religious rug out from under the feet of the orthodox Puritans. It is not surprising that they disliked and suspected and vilified him.

But Fox in his own person, as Colin Wilson has penetratingly remarked, summarized both extreme Dissent and also Dissent organized and almost institutionalized: at one end of his religious career he was as radical as any Leveller, yet at the other end he was as established a person as John Owen, Cromwell's Oxford Vice-Chancellor. After the phase of persecution at the hands of orthodox Puritans, says Wilson, 'Fox had ceased to be a Barbusse-type Outsider, a man-on-his-own in a world that did not understand him, and had become a leader of a movement that soon became thousands strong'.[23] In his own life he spanned the whole spectrum implied in the fact that 'Quakers' and 'Society of Friends' became synonymous.

9. *Coming of Age*

By the year of the Restoration, then, it may be said that the Puritan mind in England had 'come of age'. That is to say, it had graduated through its primitive enthusiasms and its adolescent eccentricities to a maturity in which it is reasonably safe to make generalizations about its character and predictions about its behaviour. Not for another two centuries are we to see any more proliferation of eccentricity; when it comes then, it comes very largely from the influence on this country of the growing-pains of the new American religion. The English Puritan mind is now furnished with what it needs, and has learnt what it wants.

In systematic theological thinking its best work has begun to appear in the writings of John Owen, the greatest of Puritan scholastics (1616–83), and Thomas Goodwin (1600–80) the greatest of Puritan theological stylists. It had attracted to itself some of the finest minds in the country, including that of John Milton (1608–74), Latin Secretary to the Commonwealth, whose Independent churchmanship and liberal politics, expressed in his prose works such as the *Areopagitica*, were a hundredfold more influential in his own day than was his poetry. It had broadened the basis of its culture to accommodate, in the Cambridge Platonists, a real wrestling with the new philosophy of Descartes and to prepare the way for an honest encounter with the new scientific insights to be given to the world by Isaac Newton. By 1660 it was a gross error to hold that the only adjective by which a Puritan could be described was the word 'narrow'. Indeed, there is, when one takes Dissent as a whole, alongside that firmness of purpose and religious assurance which are commonly associated with its classic phase, plenty of evidence of that 'breadth' which was to disorganize the doctrine of Dissent in the next century. It is commonly judged that the traditional Puritan was culturally philistine in the seventeenth century, but in fact it was precisely his hospitality to intellectual culture that two generations later left him open to the temptation to intellectual waywardness.

But the struggles of 1640–60 had taught the Puritan how to say in public terms what he wanted of Church and State, and had presented him with most of the problems of institutionalizing his faith. He had had just long enough to feel what power was like, to see himself as a potential political force, not only as a religious reformer. And there had been just time for that essentially worldly, efficient, long-headed Puritan character which was so powerful an influence in later English economic history to develop itself. As Dr Knappen has rightly shown,[24] 'unworldliness' is not an essential part of Puritan asceticism. True, there were enthusiasts who seemed to behave as though they had no connexions with this world, as certain lawyers found out to their embarrassment in such conversations as the following at the trial of William Dewsbery:

JUDGE: What is thy name?
DEWSBERY: Unknown to the world.
J.: Let us know what name that is, that the world knows not.
D.: It is known in the light, and not any can know it but him that hath it; but the name the world knows me by is William Dewsbery.
J.: What countryman art thou?
D.: Of the land of Canaan.
J.: That is afar off.
D.: Nay, it is near, for all that dwell in God are in the holy city, Jerusalem.[25]

But even there one may suspect a little pious play-acting on the part of the prisoner. What it is always unwise to forget is that character in the seventeenth-century Puritan, derived partly from his social standing in the English economic scheme of his time, which prompted Hilaire Belloc's acid remark, apropos of the Reformation views on economics, 'The regarding of it [sc. usury] as legitimate, normal and even beneficent was new, and was the product of the breakdown in the old moral authority coupled with Calvin's doctrine of man's duty to grow rich'.[26] Where the Puritan minister and the Puritan congregation had 'found themselves', there, in potentia, were the Puritan merchant, the Puritan banker and the Puritan company-promoter. Along with a quest for holiness went an achievement of bourgeois efficiency: frugality was not only godly, but it paid dividends in good health and prosperity. Licentiousness, said Doddridge delightfully, is not only impious: it is also expensive.[27] It only needed the reaffirmation of aristocratic values against bourgeois values, of Anglican ways against Puritan ways, of courtly culture against rational and liberal culture, to show the Puritans that this was indeed what they had been standing for all the time, and to confirm them in their quest for political liberty, for scriptural church order and for personal holiness.

CHAPTER VII

THE HARD WAY, 1660–1714

1. *Restoration and retaliation*

Sometimes in the school playground one may see the supposedly edifying sight of a small urchin fighting and vanquishing another boy considerably his senior in years and his superior in weight. In such a case, especially if he whose nose is rolled in the dust had some reputation for bullying, public opinion of the English sort allows itself to rejoice in the upsetting of a traditional authority, and to congratulate the impudent but valiant aggressor. Thus, on the whole, have historians and commentators in general treated the regicide Puritans generously. History has presented itself to us, softened by the passage of time, pretty much in terms of the valiant minority successfully bringing the established, the wealthy, the much-respected to their knees.

But if in that same playground the larger fellow, the representative of traditional, natural authority, gathers some of his friends round him, and satisfies them that the impudence of the aggressor was greater than his bravery, and if in consequence the small boy is on some later occasion rolled in the mud by the larger one, there will be in the larger boy's mind a certain kind of bitterness, and in his handling of the small boy a certain kind of violence that would not have been there had the circumstances not been such as to produce the temporary 'dissent' against natural authority in public opinion at large. Bold, brave and dedicated though the Ironsides were, upright and honest though the Puritans were, the Puritan violence begot in

Royalist-restoration minds a special kind of fury. Added to the natural effort of the beaten side to restore its fortunes at the expense of their sometime victors, there was this curious disgust and horror at the thought of the impudence that had brought the Puritans to their place of triumph.

Some broadly psychological explanation of that sort is the only one that will explain the extraordinary brutalities and ferocities of the Anglicans towards the Dissenters in the years immediately following the Restoration. Of these brutalities historians of Puritan mind have, of course, made the most. But the passing of nearly three centuries has enabled men to produce studies of the matter objective enough to show us that when we have said all we can in justification of either side, the treatment of Puritans by the King's men after 1660 was at no point less horrific than the treatment of Royalists by Puritans had been during the twenty years preceding; the important difference is this, that whereas Puritan violence against the Royalists and the Anglicans consisted of a series of forays against their well-prepared positions, of the ejection from their livings of Royalist-minded vicars, of packing Parliament with Puritan burghers, of snatching power local and national where it was available to be snatched, the Established violence against Puritans consisted very largely of applying the existing law, and amplifying it where necessary. From the Anglican point of view the Clarendon Code and all that went with it was a single operation calculated to restore law and order, to make examples of the disturbers of the peace, and to put back authority into the hands of those from whom it had been violently and outrageously stolen.

The enemies of the Puritans, after the Restoration, had all the weight of tradition on their side. It was not difficult for them to say in effect to the villagers and townsmen of

England, 'These fanatics are bringing the whole of law and order into disrepute. Help us to restore the greatness of England by putting them where they belong.'

The story of what actually happened is familiar enough and may be read at length in the sources.[1] Unparalleled rejoicing, under which lay a sense of profound relief, marked the Restoration of Charles II, and of the old aristocratic way of life. The Englishman enjoys the sight of authority bloody-nosed, provided the blood flows not too freely or too long. He enjoys it only because there is something else in him, something antecedent to his love of inversions, which loves a secure and settled pattern of things. Only a spiritually secure person can afford a sense of humour; and only a community with a settled axiom about political security can afford its fancy for the leg-pulling of what it regards as the 'natural authorities'. That part of Englishness which welcomes the temporary triumph of the minority welcomes it because it is temporary. It was easy for the people after 1660 to see in what danger they had stood of becoming a military dictatorship under Cromwell.

A reaction against the cruder manifestations of democracy was to be expected. The whole of English culture was deeply influenced by continental aristocratic culture in the time of the second Charles just because it had been so rudely disturbed by the democratic culture of the Puritans. Dissent suddenly looked very unpleasant indeed, and in those few days of national mafficking the modern 'church and chapel' village-mind was born in England.

2. *The Prayer-Book colloquy, 1661*

The prelude to what was to come was the Savoy Conversations of 1661, in which, by royal command, representatives of the Puritan mind and of the Church of England were

called together at the Savoy palace to consider their
differences and see whether a common mind could be
achieved. Here was an historical irony. It was little more
than two years before that at that same palace the reigning
Puritans, those of Cromwellian and Congregationalist
mind, had written and published the *Savoy Declaration of
Faith and Order*, which contained a comprehensive plan
for the new Church of England derived from the Westminster Confession.[2] The mind behind this document,
which amplified the earlier Confession and modified it
at certain theological points, was that of John Owen. It
provided for a carefully selected ministry, a federation
of local churches through synods, a clear principle of
membership with sanctions of excommunication, and
an adaptation to English needs of the Calvinist Church
system. This was to have been the charter of the English
Church. It was written in the year of Cromwell's death.
And now, within three years, the centre of discussion
is not the forgotten declaration of Savoy but the Book
of Common Prayer.

Forty-one divines met at the Savoy to hold a colloquy
about Prayer-Book revision. Of these eleven were Presbyterian divines, and their names, almost symbolically,
appear in the *Accompt* of the proceedings[3] in a group
sandwiched between the names of twelve bishops before
them, and eighteen High Church clergy after them. We must
not here examine in detail the Presbyterian contentions,[4]
but there is no better document of the educated and
developed Puritan mind than the *Exceptions Against the
Book of Common Prayer* and the specimen prayer-book
which the Puritans contributed to the discussion. Here
you see far more than you could see in the Westminster
Confession or the Savoy Declaration, in as much as

a liturgy necessarily combines theology with practice. One extended quotation will save us many pages of commentary.

Here, then, is the form for the General Confession of sin, which the Presbyterians suggested should be used on the Lord's Day at an early point in the service. Two forms are offered: this is headed by the rubric, *Or thus, when Brevity is necessary.*

O most great, most just and gracious God, thou art of purer eyes than to behold iniquity, thou condemnest the ungodly, impenitent and unbelievers; but hast promised mercy through Jesus Christ to all that repent and believe in him. We confess that we were conceived in sin, and are by nature Children of wrath. And have all sinned and come short of the glory of God. In our Baptism thou tookest us into the bond of the holy Covenant, but we remembered not our Creator in the days of our youth, with the fear, and love, and obedience which we owed thee: not pleasing, and glorifying thee in all things, nor walking with thee, by faith in an Heavenly conversation, nor serving thee fervently with all our might: but fulfilled the desires of the flesh, and of the Carnal mind. We have neglected and abused thy Holy Worship, thy Holy Name, and thy Holy Day. We have dishonoured our superiors and neglected our inferiors: We have dealt unjustly, and uncharitably, with our Neighbours, not loving them as our selves, nor doing to others as we would they should do to us, we have not sought first thy Kingdom, and Righteousness, and been contented with our daily bread, but have been careful and troubled about many things, neglecting the one thing necessary. Thou hast revealed thy wonderful love to us in Christ, and offered us pardon and salvation, in him: but we made light of it and neglected so great salvation, and resisted thy Spirit, Word and Ministers, and turned not at thy reproof. We have run into temptations; and the sin which we should have hated, we have committed in thy sight, both secretly and openly, ignorantly and carelessly, rashly, and presumptuously, against thy precepts, thy promises, and threats, thy mercies and thy judgements; our transgressions are multiplied before Thee, and our sins testify against us; if Thou deal with us as we deserve, Thou wilt cast us from thy presence into Hell, where the worm never dieth, and the fire is not quenched. But in thy mercy, thy Son, and thy Promises is our hope. Have mercy upon us most merciful Father. Be reconciled to us, and let the blood of Jesus Christ cleanse us from all our sins. Take us for thy children, and give us the Spirit of thy Son. Sanctify us wholly, shed abroad thy love in our hearts, and cause us to love Thee with all our hearts. O make thy grace to shine upon thy servants; save us from our sins, and from the wrath to come; make us a peculiar people to Thee, zealous of good works, that we may please Thee, and shew forth thy praise. Help us to redeem the time, and give all diligence to make our Calling and Election sure. Give us things necessary for thy service, and keep us from sinful discontent and cares. And seeing all these things must be dissolved, let us consider what manner of persons we ought to be, in all holy conversation and godliness. Help us to watch against temptations, and resist and overcome the Flesh, the Devil, and the World; and being delivered out of the hand of all our enemies, let us serve Thee without fear in holiness and righteousness before Thee all the days of our life. Guide us by thy Counsel, and after receive us into thy glory, through Jesus Christ our only Saviour, *Amen.*

The General Confession in the Book of Common Prayer contains 132 words: the prayer above has something like 560 words, and in the margin are placed seventy-five Scripture references. The longer form of Confession, which is presumably preferred by the compilers of the order of service, has 1300 words and 172 Scripture citations.

It is generally thought that this document, which was produced at a fortnight's notice for examination at the Savoy, is substantially a reproduction of the Sunday service at Kidderminster, where the vicar was Richard Baxter, a member of the colloquy. There is very little left to say about the development of the Puritan mind once one has closely examined and soaked oneself in a devotion of this sort. Observe its very great length, and contrast it with the brevity of Cranmer. The principle is that nothing must be omitted, that nothing must be left to the imagination. The contrary principle is that a brief and often-repeated prayer forms a serviceable basis for personal prayer arising out of it; with that Anglican contention the Puritans would have nothing to do. Observe the pains-taking manner in which every phrase reminiscent of Scripture is traced to its source, and the source noted in the margin. Scripture is the beginning and end of worship and church order for the Puritans. The Anglicans might well retort that the reminiscence of Isaiah liii. 6 at the opening of their General Confession is quite sufficient to induce a penitent mind; but for the Puritans, the more Scripture the better. Observe its total lack of style: there are exalted passages, but there is no rhythm, no attempt to avoid by graceful circumlocution or synonym a phrase like 'shed abroad thy love in our hearts, and cause us to love thee with all our hearts'. Puritan honesty usually ran to an excess of literalism. Graceful turns of phrase were to them a means of hiding the real meaning, or of blurring the urgent sense, of what was being said.

No, said the Puritans. We must express in our public worship our sense of the need of holiness, our devotion to Scripture, and our conviction that man comes freely to God without priestly intervention. We must make our prayers as personal, and as little priestly, as we can, preferring that crudity which comes from Scripture to that urbanity which smacks to us of 'the church'.

I am sure that a document of this kind is more important to the present study than an examination of documents of church order, precisely because we see in the habits of Christians at worship the real perplexities that confront anybody who seeks to analyse the motives of Christian politics. It is when one Christian goes to attend worship at the church of another kind of Christian that the affections play havoc with the reason, not when Christians of different denominations sit at a table discussing church order. Worship involves not merely reason and principles of good order, but (whatever its form) rhetoric and aesthetic as well. Where a public act of worship is proceeding, you are involved not only with matters of correctness and routine, but also with the effect of words uttered by one person on a small or large number of hearers. Whatever the intentions of those who order the act of worship, that effect will be immediate, and the result in the worshipper's mind is to create at once an *ethos*, as well as a theory of worship. In the end, then, any given Christian, when considering different forms of worship, is inevitably much moved by the proposition, 'I don't like that kind of worship'; and if by any chance there is a controversy going on around him, he is unable to avoid proceeding to the proposition, 'I don't like the kind of person who likes that kind of worship'.

If the reader then looks carefully at the prayer, imagines it being said in a church by a minister, and asks himself what kind of person would compose it, and what kind of person would approve it, he will more quickly than by any other means find himself 'existentially' involved in the controversy of 1661–2. He will be himself on one side or on the other, and that is where he must be if the movements of the denominations between that age and this are to be intelligible to him. We may here suggest that the kind of person to whom a Confession of that kind seems the appropriate way of worship is he who prefers the concept to the image, the clearly stated to the suggested, plain speech before good manners, personal intimacy before ceremoniousness. He is of those to whom it comes naturally to speak at all seasons in religious terms; he is morally perfectionist and unwilling to accept, or to admit that he accepts, moral compromise. He believes in the communication of religious thought and feeling through extended and carefully ordered monologue rather than through the conversation and action of church liturgy. He is likely to take more notice of the sermon than of the sacraments. He is of those who prefer that every Sunday the whole truth be set forth, and who dislike seasonal celebrations and local emphases. He insists on personal rectitude, has a very high sense of the majesty of God's action in rescuing mankind from that everlasting punishment which he deserves, and therefore is slow to praise men but quick to praise God.

This, of course, was 'right wing' Puritanism. This was the Presbyterian mind. There were plenty of Puritans, of the Independent or neo-Anabaptist sort, who would have thought it profanity to commit any kind of prayer to paper, and a popish bondage to prescribe any kind of liturgy whatever. These were, in a sense, almost more consistent than the Presbyterians, for one is bound to judge that Baxter's prayers look like nothing so much as extemporary prayers hastily transcribed. It was not of the 'left wing' Puritan mind to go so carefully as did the Presbyterians into the details of the Book of Common Prayer, nor to make such minute suggestions in respect of rubrics and texts. They would have preferred simply to say that any kind of directory of worship was 'of the Old Covenant' and not proper to the New Age of spiritual freedom.

What might have happened had the Savoy Colloquy been convened by Cromwell seven years before, we cannot here stop to suggest. What did happen was that the conference broke down in acrimonious disorder, and the prevailing impression that one gathers from reading its extensive papers is of the bishops and High-churchmen saying to each other after the Puritans had left the room,

'You see? That is what we knew they would say. They are quite impossible. There is only one thing to do with people like that.' And the Presbyterians said the same. Both, we may be sure, included in their comments the contemporary equivalent of 'people like that'. That was the heart of it. At the highest level, real hatred and vindictiveness were generated by this collision between the late victors and the late vanquished.

3. *Ejection*

On 19 May 1662 the Act of Uniformity received the royal assent. In its preamble Parliament expressed its disgust at the confusion wrought by nonconformity in English religion. 'A great Number of People, in divers Parts of this Realm, following their own Sensuality, and living without Knowledge and due Fear of God, do wilfully and schismatically abstain and refuse to come to their parish Churches and other Places where Common Prayer, Administration of the Sacraments, and Preaching of the Word of God is used.'[5] This having led to 'the great decay and scandal of the reformed religion of the Church of England, and to the hazard of many souls', it was enacted that the Book of Common Prayer, as recently revised (1662), be alone and by authority used and read by 'all and singular ministers in any cathedral, collegiate or parish Church or Chapel, or other place of Worship within this Realm of England, dominion of Wales, and town of Berwick-upon-Tweed'. Further, it was required of every minister that at some date between 19 May and 24 August 1662 he should solemnly read the services of the Prayer Book in his church, and with them a declaration of 'unfeigned assent and consent to all and everything contained and prescribed in and by the book entitled, the Book of

Common Prayer'. Failure to obey this enactment would bring at once the deprivation of all 'spiritual promotions'. Should any person holding an incumbency, but not being in Holy Episcopal Orders, not become episcopally ordained by that same date, 24 August, 'he shall be utterly disabled, and all his ecclesiastical Promotions shall be void, as if he was naturally dead'.

Those words of offended dignity ushered in the period of persecution. By them the promise of the Declaration of Breda, given under the new king's hand, in the words 'we do declare a liberty to tender consciences, and that no man shall be disquieted or called in question for differences of opinion in matter of religion' was formally set aside. It was all very well for a new sovereign to appear benevolent towards religious sectaries before he had even set foot in the country as king, but no member of the new Parliament really believed that a man could refuse conformity and still profess loyalty to the Crown. By the Corporation Act of May 1661 the Solemn League and Covenant was declared void, and the appointment of High-churchmen to public office was restored; it was too much to expect otherwise than that this should be done by a positive requirement that 'no person shall for ever hereafter be placed... in any of the offices or places aforesaid that shall not have, within one year next before such election or choice, taken the Sacrament of the Lord's Supper according to the Rites of the Church of England'.

That had already been enacted. The decisive blow was, however, the Act of Uniformity which at once drove two thousand incumbents from their livings, and left them, so far as ecclesiastical livelihood went, destitute.

At once and naturally, such ministers as declined to subscribe to the Prayer Book began to form their own congregations. Under the Act these were illegal; but a series of further Acts was brought into operation in order that their illegality might be precisely defined. Under the Conventicle Act (1664) any person above the age of sixteen attending any nonconformist act of worship at which more than five persons were present was liable to a fine of £5 for the first offence, of £10 for the second, with the alternative of six months in gaol, and of £100 for the third, with the alternative of transportation. (Ingeniously, the Act provided that the transportation, which was to last seven years, must not be to Virginia or New England, where nonconformity had already made itself a comfortable home.)

Under the Five Mile Act (30 October 1665) it was provided that no person who had been found preaching in an unlawful conventicle must thereafter be found within five miles of any 'city or town corporate, or borough that sends burgesses to Parliament'. The result of this was the foundation of numerous congregations in remote country villages, many of which have continued to the present day with an unbroken ministerial succession.

Those four Acts constitute what is commonly called the 'Clarendon Code', and life for Dissenting ministers and their elders and people was extremely hazardous during the first decade of the Restoration. A curious respite was offered to the nonconformists in 1672 when, in order to gain favour with the many businessmen among nonconformists whose support would be valuable to him in the alliance with Louis XIV against Holland (against which public opinion was mounting), Charles II issued a Declaration of Indulgence. This Declaration was unconstitutional, and any comfort it brought to the nonconformists was much modified by the affront it presented to their consciences. Parliament reversed it in 1673 by passing a second Conventicle Act, reaffirming the terms of the former which some thought to have expired with the previous Parliament, and rehabilitating that anti-nonconformist opinion to which the fall of Clarendon (1667) had dealt a shrewd blow. The penalties attached to this second Conventicle Act were less stringent than those prescribed in the first; but its terms of reference were wider, and permitted the virtually indiscriminate harrying of all who would not subscribe. In 1673 also the Test Act, primarily designed as a gesture against Roman Catholics and providing that all persons in Crown employment, civil or military, must receive the Lord's Supper in the Anglican form, sign a declaration against Transubstantiation, and take the oaths of Allegiance and Supremacy, reinforced upon nonconformists (and, of course, on Catholics) the burdens of the earlier Corporation Act.

This was a better-organized and less bloody version of 1593. Once again, Dissent was treasonable in that an oath of allegiance to the sovereign was at every point added to the subscriptions required of all who wished to escape persecution; but it was not treason of a kind thought to be punishable by death. Politics and religion were now much more inextricably mixed than they had been in the days of Penry and Greenwood. It is a good guide to the difference between the climates of the two periods to recognize that whereas in the 1593 period we talk historically of Dissent, in the 1662 period we talk of nonconformity. In 1593 Barrow and Greenwood could have escaped by signing a confession admitting their treasonable activities and pledging themselves to loyalty to the Queen; in 1662 any nonconformist could escape by going to his parish church and receiving Communion.

To put it otherwise: in 1593, to escape the wrath of authority, a Dissenter had to confess to having done what he had not done. In 1662 he must simply conform. In 1662 it was purely a conscientious matter, and the punishment he avoided was not death or life-imprisonment (although if he were contumacious in breaking the law the prison would welcome him), but the loss of livelihood, and the silencing of his prophetic voice.

But contumacious the nonconformists were, and the prisons began to fill up. History shows us numerous tiny congregations of the faithful Puritans meeting in places as obscure as they could find—in the middle of a field, that pursuers might easily be seen coming; in a hay-loft; in a cellar; or in the large house of some wealthy merchant who could afford the fines. It was a very disagreeable aspect of this legislation (as of most legislation of the period) that you could always buy your way out of prison if you could afford it. There was more than one distinguished Englishman who could say in 1689 that he had spent ten thousand pounds on fines for personal or congregational nonconformity.

If the fine could not be paid, prison was the alternative, and many harrowing stories can be read of the manner in which the nonconformists suffered in the crowded prisons of the county towns.[6] Ministers were often saved from prison or from destitution by the benevolence of their congregations: but not infrequently a minister was unlucky in having a small and poor congregation, or suffered imprisonment, refusing to have his fine paid, for the sake of his conscience.

The efficiency of the administration of penal laws against nonconformity was always modified by the public opinion in a village, or by some special circumstance in the offender's personal case. Bunyan lay in Bedford prison (and, to be sure, improved his time), but John Owen and Edmund Calamy preached widely and were little molested. Chief Justice Jeffreys treated his prisoners according to the personal impression they made on him: Philip Henry he loved, Richard Baxter he hated.[7] One magistrate differed widely from another in the weight of the burden he laid on those he sentenced; and a great deal depended on the temperament of the individual gaoler into whose hands the prisoner might fall. There were hideous brutalities here, and unexpected leniencies there.

What matters is not to assess the precise measure of injustice and cruelty that accompanied this persecution, but to be clear about the effect that it had on nonconformity in England. There can be little doubt that had the authorities deliberately planned to organize a persecution just pernicious enough to settle a habit of righteous indignation in nonconformity, but not violent enough to crush it completely, they could hardly have succeeded better. Nonconformity positively flourished and grew in stature during the years of its trial. The individual suffering involved was enough to inspire the movement and to shame the doubters, but it was not so ultimate as to extinguish hope, nor so universally imposed as to leave no chance for the Puritan spirit to nourish itself.

In the days of persecution, then, Puritanism became a way of life based strictly on family worship and family loyalty. It had always been that to some extent: indeed, the real inspiration that the Puritans gained from the persecution was perhaps the discovery how many of their ancient contentions turned out to be unexpectedly right and practical. Simple and unadorned worship—what more can you have, and what more do you want, in a hay-loft? Honesty and personal integrity—what less will keep you going under emergency conditions? Separation from State power—that has been achieved for us by the State itself. Biblical religion based on sermons—what ecclesiastical gear can we carry about with us from one barn to the next except a Bible, and what can we better do than gather round it a dozen or half a dozen at a time? As for church authority, why, it is the pestilent Dissenters, the Independents, the Congregationalists, who have the right of it after all, for what, in times like these, can we make of presbyteries, let alone bishops? It is hand-to-mouth warfare, each small detachment having to make its own decisions.

So the thoughts of any Puritan religious who had time to think may well have run. Gone, and so far as he could see gone for ever, were the days when men of the Puritan mind could hope for anything in this world. Cromwell's Commonwealth was hardly mentioned. Sufficient for the day was the evil thereof.

There is no figure who typifies the English Dissent of the later seventeenth century so well, surely, as Richard Baxter.

4. *Baxter and Bunyan*

Baxter (1615–91), a Shropshire boy whose youth was burdened by ill health probably of a nervous kind, was ordained by the Bishop of Worcester in 1638, and spent two years as Master of the Free Grammar School at Bridgnorth. In 1640 he made up his mind to reject Episcopacy and throw in his lot with the Puritans. From 1641 to 1660 he was curate at Kidderminster, and from 1660 onwards he held the incumbency.

Baxter is a new kind of Puritan. He was in no sense

politically radical: indeed, his political writings show him
to be quite astonishingly intolerant of anything like popular
or democratic government.[8] He was first and last an
ecclesiastical statesman and a pastor, interested in nothing
whatever that was not strictly of the Church. He was
Presbyterian by habit, because Presbyterianism was in a
majority when he joined the Puritan party: but he has
nothing to say about church order, as between Presbyterian
and Independent, and very little to say directly about the
obliquity of episcopal government.

But despite this he is the most voluminous of all classic
Puritan writers. Something like two hundred books came
from his indefatigable pen. Of the 159 works mentioned
in a list compiled by Alexander Grosart[9] very much more
than half are works of spiritual counsel; Baxter wrote all
his sermons and republished them in the form of extended
tracts on such subjects as *Of Justification: Four Disputa-
tions* (1658), *Directions and Perswasions to a Sound Conversion* (1660), *Directions for Weak distempered Christians
to Grow up to a confirmed State of Grace* (1669)—not to
mention the *Reformed Pastor* (1656). Where he writes of
the Church he writes primarily of the Church's unity,
saving his polemics for the 'vanity of Papists and all
schismaticks that confine the Catholick Church to their
own sect'—a phrase from the title of a 275-page book of
his dated 1660. Baxter was, in fact, conventional to the
point of Toryism in all things but church matters. His
pastoral advice to his flock, of which we can read thousands of pages in his extant works, was codified and categorized with astonishing care. He was a great lover of the
tabular technique: the sins against which he was preaching,
or the remedies for them, were regularly categorized in
tables of twelve heads, or twenty, or two dozen, or fifty.

His mind was exceedingly clear, but his approach to realities had a touch of the obsessive about it, a touch of the spiritual pedant. It was very probably his legalistic pedantries that exacerbated Jeffreys; a judge of his kind would find no prisoner more intolerable than one with a clear and pernickety lawyer's mind.

In Baxter we see the change from Puritanism militant, Puritanism sparkling with originality and intellectual Dissent as well as frowning with ecclesiastical Dissent, to Puritanism inward-looking and spiritually technical. Baxter, indeed, is the first of the Puritans in any way to resemble the popular image of 'the Puritan'. Bishop Henson's comment on Baxter, though displeasing to Baxter's best friends, is a just comment on a certain kind of Puritan piety:

I...think that Baxter was almost morbidly self-centred, and his self-analysis, which expresses a genuine humility, does also indicate this unwholesome and excessive interest in himself. Among his great endowments of head and heart there was not included what is commonly called a sense of humour. That precious (but uncommon) quality enables a man to 'see himself as others see him', and thus to escape the rigidity of attitude and judgment which disfigures so many admirably good people, and among them, I think, Baxter. I do not think he could have produced his Prayer Book at the Savoy Conference, if he had had a sense of humour. The circumstances of his education, his chronic ill-health, and the untoward course of his life stimulated the natural egotism which he possessed; and, I think, no one can read his writings without feeling that he was a man who took little heed to the counsels of others, and ever sought to bring the wayward mystery of human life into the frame of theory.[10]

Those words were written by a discerning critic of the human spirit who had read widely in Baxter; and they are just. For persecution may bring out in one sense the best in a persecuted community—the best in the way of courage, resource and endurance; but history invariably

shows that a degree of self-interest goes with that courage
—self-interest, that is, in a proper context, a reasonable self-
preservation. It is not easy for a community under persecution, and it is even less easy for a free community lately
persecuted, to take that interest in other communities
which is necessary for its complete health.

Puritanism at its very best, Puritanism distinguished by
virtues it did not often give rise to, is in John Bunyan
(1628–88), Baxter's contemporary. Bunyan the Bedford
brazier knew about 'the world'; he knew of Dissent not
only as dissent from episcopacy but as dissent from the
devil. *Grace Abounding*, his autobiography, is little more
merry, and yet much more robust, than Baxter's autobiography; and as for *The Pilgrim's Progress*, what other
written work from the English Puritans is to be compared
with it? With Milton, Bunyan has the poet's earthy simplicity; Bunyan can break through the conventional
lecture and sermon technique of Puritanism and give his
dogmas flesh and blood. Bunyan is the only one of all
these laborious and devoted men who dared to see Despair
as a bog, and Heaven as the Bedfordshire hills; that is as
much as to say that Bunyan alone of them all—not even
Milton excepted—was fully human in his vision of Calvin's
doctrine. It is difficult to be too grateful for Bunyan. Few
of the Puritan authors seem to have had the least patience
with their audience or reader; it occurred to few of them
(though here I should often except Goodwin) that their
reader might be profoundly bored by them. Men (they
assumed) should not be, and therefore are not, bored by
sacred things. Bunyan was lifted above that pious arro-
gance when he wrote about his pilgrim.

5. *Toleration*

The years during which nonconformity was under official persecution were years of swift and significant political development in England. Few monarchs before his time made a contribution to the life of their country more distinguished and yet more morally ambivalent than was the contribution of Charles II. Personally, Charles was the incarnation of the opposite of all Puritan values; sociable, spendthrift, promiscuous and excellent company. He and his court stood for values which the Puritans found easy to hold in contempt. Yet although so much that Charles did was unconstitutional, there was never any thought that 1649 would repeat itself. Public opinion was reasonably sure that tyranny would not again and so soon appear in this country.

An important development during the second half of the seventeenth century was the marked increase in the political literacy of the country as a whole. The chief instrument of this was the news-letter, a device of private correspondence from London to the country which circumvented an accepted censorship that made newspapers of the modern kind impossible. The news-letter, privately hand-written, but regarded at its point of receipt as available for the neighbours to read, was a tangential development of the political pamphlet which had so much to do with the Reformation both abroad and in England.[11] It was one sign among many that the people, after the revolution of 1640–60, were becoming in a new way conscious of a democratic heritage and of the necessity for parliamentary vigilance. It was perhaps for reasons of this kind that Charles's gesture of toleration in 1672 was so abruptly reversed the next year by his Parliament.

At any rate, Charles succeeded in making himself a popular sovereign at all points except in the fact that privately he professed the Roman Catholic Faith. The reasons for this were closely connected with his desire for alliance with the French king (Louis XIV); an alliance into which he entered somewhat furtively at Dover in 1670 at the expense of the Dutch alliance that had persisted for so long. This was a clear move from Protestantism towards Catholicism, and its repercussions in England were to give this country for a short season a taste of that terrible warfare between Catholic and Protestant which had wrought such spiritual havoc on the Continent between 1560 and 1598 and during the Thirty Years War of 1618–48.

The red light, then, was showing before Charles II died, and English opinion was ready for open controversy with the Catholics. Then, in the year of Charles's death, 1685, Louis XIV revoked the Edict of Nantes. It was a gesture calculated to gain the sympathy of Charles II; by the edict of Nantes (1598) a measure of toleration had been granted to the Huguenots, who represented in France both the religious interests and the social forces which Puritanism represented in England. Agreeable though it was to Charles's religious sense, it was, as a gesture of respect towards England, a lunatic miscalculation. Not only was England firmly Protestant by now—for at every point the middle-of-the-road Englishman feared Rome as much as he despised Geneva—but the Huguenots promptly made their way out of France to Britain, and strengthened the already formidable Protestant feeling that they found here.

On the death of Charles, King James II began without delay to make it clear that whereas Charles had been a conforming but not demonstrative Catholic, his own

Catholic faith was of the positive and soul-compelling sort. Where Charles had not considered any steps towards making England a Catholic country, James reckoned that his work would not be well done if England remained a Protestant one. But acts which to him appeared strictly religious were interpreted, justifiably, by his ministers as unconstitutional, and after three years his reign was ended in what Protestant English history has always called the 'Glorious Revolution' of 1688: 'glorious because it was bloodless', says Fisher in one place, 'glorious because it was clement' in another.[12]

The Revolution was a decisive Protestant gesture, and thrust English politics in the Whig direction, and English religion in the direction of Puritanism. On the accession of William of Orange, who was nothing if not an example of the duller Puritan virtues, an act of toleration putting an end to the persecution of orthodox Dissent in England was bound to come. It was in fact passed, almost unopposed, on 24 May 1689.

This Act of Toleration, be it observed, was not a literal repeal of the Clarendon Code. There was nothing in it to give hope to any who still looked for a Calvinist and Presbyterian Church of England. It was in part a rationalizing and civilizing of much that had already taken place. It provided, to be precise, for the repeal of the ancient Elizabethan order that made it legal to levy fines on Dissenters for failure to attend their parish church, and for the withdrawal of all power to prosecute Dissenters, whether Protestant or Catholic, merely for their Dissent. But it did not in so many words declare the Corporation Act, the Act of Uniformity, the Conventicle Acts, the Five Mile Act and the Test Act void; nor did it remove from Dissenters those political and social disabilities which the

Clarendon Code had laid on them. In the Act of Toleration it was provided that if a man was elected to a public
office, but scrupled to take the oath associated with it by
the Corporation Act, he might be permitted to act through
a deputy. Under persecution it was possible maliciously
to elect a known Dissenter to public office, and then to
collect from him a substantial fine both for his Dissent
and for his refusing to take the oath and the office to which
it was attached. Unhappily the Act of Toleration only
specified certain minor offices under this head—those of
'high-constable, or petit-constable, churchwarden, over-
seer of the poor, or any other parochial or ward-office'.
It therefore remained possible, in respect of such offices as
the Lord Mayoralty of London, for the disagreeable
practice of appointing and penalizing known Dissenters to
continue; and as we shall see, it did continue.

Dissenters had hoped for more than toleration. They
had looked for 'comprehension', which would have meant
their being fully taken into the system of the Church of
England. Nobody now expected the Church of England
to follow the pattern of the Westminster Confession, but
it was greatly hoped in some quarters that a place for
Dissent would be made within the Church of England,
and not just outside it. Although toleration did remove
the worst abuses of the Clarendon Code, what really
happened was, in modern terms, the substitution of 'cold
war' for 'shooting war'. Tolerated they were, but very far
from generally liked or respected or understood; and
therefore Dissent had to face problems altogether more
complex and elusive, because less immediately painful,
than those the previous generation had faced with such
intrepidity. They had to learn to live at peace with men who
refrained from persecution, but not from contempt.

The climate of England during the reign of William III was, of course, Whig, progressive, and religiously tolerant of all except Roman Catholics. But the equilibrium was far from stable. On the death of William III, 8 March 1702, the hopes of Dissenters were shaken by the prospect of what might be the policy of his successor, Queen Anne; for Anne was favourable to the Tory interest and the High Church party, and the quick replacement of Whigs by Tories in key-positions in politics in the early months of Anne's reign was for Dissenters a bad sign.

6. *Early setbacks*

For despite the official toleration—perhaps partly because of it—Dissenters were no more loved in the last few years of the seventeenth century than they had been in the decades of persecution. Probably they were less loved. The small boy, once suitably chastised and restrained, is offensive to his superiors in a manner different from the offensiveness of the same small boy when he picks himself up again and is granted by the authorities a measure of rehabilitation. During the days of persecution, alongside the legal violence, there continued at high levels a dignified debate between the Dissenting and Anglican interests which is recorded in a long series of books and pamphlets. There is a famous pair of volumes entitled *A Collection of Cases and Other Discourses Lately Written to Recover Dissenters to the Communion of the Church of England*, published in 1685; these two books contain about 1500 pages between them, representing twenty-three discourses averaging sixty-five pages each, all delivered by Anglican dignitaries to the purpose of recovering the Dissenters by reason where it seemed that the Church was failing to recover them by force. This is but one phase of the controversy, and but one side of it. Allocutions of this kind could be delivered in a spirit of slightly patronizing generosity when their subjects were religiously outlawed: it was kinder to talk than to fine and imprison.

But once the prisons emptied and Dissenters began to walk freely and worship openly, a new spirit may be expected in the Anglican persuasiveness, and nowhere is this spirit more completely evidenced than in the speeches and writings of Dr Henry Sacheverell, Fellow of Magdalen College, Oxford, and later chaplain of St Saviour's, Southwark.

Sacheverell, who died in 1724 and is supposed to have been born about 1674, preached a sermon at Oxford denouncing those churchmen who had favoured the toleration of Dissenters. This was in 1702, when he was still hardly thirty years old. Oxford has always been (indeed, it remains) a place where the Dissenting interest has had short shrift, and Sacheverell represented a fair body of local and national opinion when he deemed the University church a proper place for an attack on the whole principle of the Toleration Act. Those who favoured it he called 'apostates', and the principle of it he described as 'an amazing contradiction of our reason'.

His attack was answered by Daniel Defoe in a bitterly ironic satire, *The Shortest Way with Dissenters*, which brought its author before the magistrates. He was fined, imprisoned, and stood three times in the pillory, but the people cheered him and drank his health, for that Whiggery and religious progressivism upon which the new queen frowned was still popular with the ordinary Englishman. The pamphlet was more popular with the uncommitted than with the protagonists in the controversy, for there were many of the graver Dissenting leaders who shook their heads at the thought that such scurrility should be used in their defence.

Sacheverell ploughed on. In 1709 he preached before the assize at Derby, and before the Lord Mayor of London, expressing such sentiments as that the Dissenters were 'filthy dreamers and despisers of dominion', who would 'renounce their creed and recite the Decalogue backwards'; but he had reckoned without the change of government that had brought the Whigs back to power, and he was impeached and found guilty of treason to the government. He was sentenced (23 March 1710) to three years' inhibition from his clerical privileges, and his two sermons were burnt by the public hangman. This was, in effect, an award of a farthing damages. The majority against him was but 69 to 52. It is somewhat sharply to be contrasted with the treatment of Defoe a few years before.

This curious incident leaves us with the impression that in the matter of toleration, opinion in the country was somewhat finely balanced. That was to be expected. Dissenters were still very much a minority; but being the kind of people they were—not often nobly born, but uncannily successful and not infrequently wealthy—they had plenty of influence. They had lately emerged from a situation in which the uncommitted observer could easily ascribe heroism to them. They represented an interest very much in line with that interest which had deposed King James.

But just because their influence was so rapidly increasing, they were a great menace to the Tory High-churchmen, and it was not difficult for men of Tory mind to represent them as a menace to the stability and peace of the country. Therefore both Defoe and Sacheverell got a hearing. At

... shall upon every Lordes Day, and upon all other dayes and tymes
at the tymes thereui appointed dei comon and solemnly read in
all and every Ministre ... in every church, chappell or
other place of publique worshippe within this Realme of England
and Wales aforesaid ...

publique Worshippe of God (which is soe much desired) may bee
speedily effected. Bee it further enacted by the authority aforesaid
that every Parson, Vicar, or other Minister whatsoever who now hath
and enioyeth any Ecclesiasticall Benefice or promotion within the
Realme of England or place aforesaid shall in the church chappell
or place of publique Worshippe belonging to the said Benefice
or promotion, upon some Lordes Day before the feast of St
Bartholomew ... which shall bee in the yeare of
our Lord God One thousand Six hundred sixty and two openly
... and solemnly read the morning and evening prayer
appointed to bee read by and according to the said Booke of
Common Prayer at the tymes thereby appointed, and after such
reading thereof shall openly and publiquely before the Congregation
there assembled, declare his unfeigned assent and consent to the
use of all thinges ... conteyned and prescribed, And that all
and every such person who shall, without some lawfull impediment
to bee allowed, and approved of, by the Ordinary of the place,
neglect or refuse to doe the same, within the time aforesaid,
or in case of such impediment within one month after such
impediment removed, shall ipso facto bee deprived of all his
spirituall promotions, And that from thenceforth it shall bee
lawfull to and for all Patrons and Donors of all and singular the
said spirituall promotions or of any of them aceding to their
respective Rights and titles to present or Collate to the same
as though the person or persons soe offending or neglecting
were dead. And bee it further Enacted by the authority
aforesaid that every person who shall hereafter bee presented or
Collated or putt into any Ecclesiasticall Benefice or Promotion
within this Realme of England and place aforesaid, shall in the
church chappell or place of publique Worshippe belonging to the said
Benefice or Promotion, within two monethes next after that hee
shall bee in the actuall possession of the said Ecclesiasticall benefice
or promotion, upon some Lordes Day, openly publiquely and solemnly
read the morning and evening Prayere appointed to bee read
... by and according to the said Booke of Common
Prayer at the tymes thereby appointed, and after such reading
thereof shall openly and publiquely before the Congregation there
assembled declare his unfeigned assent and consent, to the use of all
thinges therein conteyned and prescribed, And that all and every such
person who shall (without some lawfull impediment to bee allowed
and approved ... by the Ordinary of the place) neglect or refuse
to doe the same within the tymes aforesaid ...

9   An extract from the Act of Uniformity

10*a* Judge Jeffreys

10*b* John Bunyan

the trials of both great crowds gathered. At Defoe's, the mob tended to drink the health of a maligned sportsman; at Sacheverell's they tended to sack the meeting-houses (five in London had their furniture thrown into the street and burnt). Defoe was, to their mind, right in a way; Sacheverell, why, yes, he was right too. But in the end Defoe was rehabilitated and spared to write *Robinson Crusoe*, while Sacheverell earned this judgement from a brother Anglican, Gilbert Burnet, bishop of Salisbury, that he was 'a bold, insolent man, with a very small measure of religion, virtue, learning or good sense who resolved to force himself into popularity and preferment by the most petulant ravings at Dissenters and low-churchman'.[13]

In this church situation there are many complexities into which it is not our business here to inquire. It must not be overlooked, for example, that the Church of England was greatly divided within itself concerning its political allegiance. In 1689 eight bishops, about 400 priests and a few laymen refused to take the Oath of Allegiance to William of Orange, believing that to do so would be a breach of that Oath which they had taken to James II (who was, of course, still alive). These 'Non-jurors', as they are called, had reason on their side, but they were at once deprived, and formed a pocket of dissent within the Anglican communion. (Among the bishops who thus resigned their sees were William Sancroft, archbishop of Canterbury, and Thomas Ken, bishop of Bath and Wells, the hymn-writer.) In their general *ethos* the nonjurors were Tractarians before their time, and in their politics they were suspected during the first half of the eighteenth century of favouring a Stuart restoration; for a time they formed separate congregations and even consecrated separated bishops, but they were gradually reabsorbed into the communion of the Church of England.

Clearly from such sources as that would come a powerful underground force acting on public opinion against the post-1689 State dispensation. But this was a cross-current, not the main stream. What really provided Sacheverell with a target to shoot at was the practice, and the legality, of 'Occasional Conformity'.

It will be recalled that under the Corporation and Test Acts attendance at a Communion service according to the Anglican rite was a necessary qualification for any public office, and that Dissenters happened to number among themselves many people who were in all other ways eminent candidates for such office. Under persecution, attendance at any Dissenting place of worship would have been a disqualification, but under Toleration it was permitted that if any man consented *pro forma* to attend such a service, he would, though an habitual Dissenter, be deemed fit for office.

The whole scheme could hardly be more religiously squalid. It was open to attack from either side. A truly faithful Dissenter would have been as disgusted as a faithful Anglican at the notion of making this sacred ordinance a key-point in qualifying for worldly advancement. But after 1689 many Dissenters availed themselves of the privilege of 'Occasional Conformity', though many others would have none of it. Isaac Watts, the hymn-writer, would not 'conform' in order to qualify for entrance to a university; his eminent patron, Sir Thomas Abney, did 'conform', in order to become Lord Mayor of London.

A man of Sacheverell's mind, however, taking a very high tone concerning the ordinances of the Church, could easily make out a case against the government for permitting such a sacrilege. His case was that the privilege of occasional conformity should at once be withdrawn, that Dissenters might be brought to their senses. The Dissenter would have said that the burden of occasional conformity should be lifted, that the Anglicans might be seen to show charity. In any case it was a repulsive abuse. But it did make it possible for Dissenters who availed themselves of it to do themselves justice in the public service, and its introduction was the last stage but one in the establishment of Dissent as a tolerated English Institution.

7. *Queen Anne's dead*

The final stage sums itself up in a quaint English proverb—'Queen Anne's dead'. The death of this exceedingly commonplace monarch was the most dramatic episode of her reign. On 12 May 1714 one Sir William Windham introduced into the House of Commons a 'Bill to Prevent the Growth of Schism', which was to provide that no person should be licensed to teach, or to keep a private school, whose conformity was not assured by subscription to an oath. That is to say—no Dissenter may teach either in a school of his own or in any school owned by another. The Bill was passed, and was to come into force as law on 1 August, which was a Sunday.

On that Sunday morning, two eminent divines met one another in the City of London. One was Bishop Burnet on his way to the Palace, the other Thomas Bradbury on his way to preach at the Independent Church in Fetter Lane. The bishop greeted the Dissenter with the remark that Bradbury was looking unusually grave. Bradbury replied, 'I am thinking, whether I shall have the constancy and resolution of that noble company of martyrs whose ashes are deposited in this place [*sc*. Smithfield]; for I most

assuredly expect to see similar times of violence and persecution, and that I shall be called to suffer in a like cause'.
The bishop then said that he was on his way to see the
Queen, who lay dying, and he promised to send a message
direct to Fetter Lane if the Queen died while he was there.
The message came, while Bradbury was preaching his
sermon. The messenger walked into the gallery of the
church and dropped a handkerchief as a sign that the
Queen was dead. Bradbury continued his sermon to the
end, but in his closing prayer invoked blessing on 'George,
King of Great Britain and Ireland'. The dispersing con-
gregation had but one thought in their minds: 'Queen
Anne's dead'—for it meant that Windham's pernicious
Bill too was dead, and that Dissenters could live in peace.[14]
A little later a deputation of a hundred ministers in black
gowns presented a loyal address to the King, Bradbury
among them. A fashionably dressed nobleman asked
Bradbury, 'What's this? A funeral?' 'Yes, my lord,' said
Bradbury, 'the funeral of the Schism Bill and the resur-
rection of Liberty.'[15]

That was the final stage. Queen Anne was dead.
A century and a half yet before there would be any thought
of religious equality, but it was the end of repression, and
measures towards it that might be attempted after this
were never able to gather the necessary weight of public
support. As for the royal influence in church affairs, the
king whose first proclamation came from a Dissenting
pulpit in London was a German who knew little English.

CHAPTER VIII

ADJUSTMENT TO TOLERATION, 1714–89

1. *Respectability*

It will be well at this point, both for historical completeness and also in order that the balance of this study may be preserved, to look back over that period of classic Dissent which the last two chapters have covered. In a learned and penetrating book, the most eminent of the present generation of Dissenting historians, Dr Geoffrey Nuttall, analyses the guiding principles of classic Dissent (the period 1640–60) under four heads: the principle of Separation, the principle of Fellowship, the principle of Freedom, and the principle of Fitness. It is just because that analysis differs somewhat from that on which the argument of this present essay is based that I wish here to refer the reader to it. Undoubtedly it is an excellent analysis of the classic Dissenting *ethos*, which is Dr Nuttall's subject. The Dissenters in their most inventive and adventurous days, in the days when they still had the vision of a Church of England which was entirely a company (to use a phrase from William Bartlet which Dr Nuttall uses as the title of his book) of 'Visible Saints', were committed to a separation that should enable them to speak clearly to society, a fellowship that would preserve the principle of charity and intimacy within the Church, a freedom that would enable Christians to learn the techniques of Christian obedience (in as much as 'his service is perfect freedom'), and a 'fitness' that should be achieved by that evangelical moral fastidiousness which takes seriously and even literally the gospel command, 'Be ye holy'.

That was the essence of Dissent, and Dr Nuttall's claim that this *ethos* is most completely exemplified in the early Independents, or Congregationalists, and that it prompted their dissent even from the Presbyterians, cannot seriously be challenged by any except the Quakers, who came into being as a society right at the end of the period he is concerned with.[1]

On the day of Queen Anne's accession in 1702, a young minister named Isaac Watts, whose name was to become the best known in the history of Independency through his hymns, became the minister at Mark Lane chapel in the City of London. A paragraph from a recent biography of Watts well describes this congregation:

The meeting in Mark Lane was one of London's most exclusive congregations. It had been founded probably in 1662 by Joseph Caryl, the author of the famous *Commentary on the Book of Job*. Caryl, dying in 1673, had been succeeded by John Owen, the acknowledged leader of Commonwealth and Restoration Independency. Under the pastorship of the latter, Mark Lane became the most aristocratic dissenting meeting in London. Among its members were Sir Thomas Overbury, Sir John Hartopp, Lady Thompson, the Countess of Anglesey, Lady Vere Wilkinson, and the remnant of the Cromwellian clan—Lord Charles Fleetwood, Major-General Desborough (Cromwell's brother-in-law), Major-General Berry, and Mrs Bendish, Cromwell's eccentric and 'enthusiastic' granddaughter.[2]

Some of these eminent persons had died by the time Watts took up his ministry there; but in his time there were the family of Sir Thomas Abney, the widow of Edward Polhill of the 'Kentish Petition', and a branch of the Shute family including the first Lord Barrington. Two Lord Mayors, and three M.P.s are in that list. Lawyers and influential businessmen and landed gentry of the newer sort packed his church, and they expected a learned ministry; Sir John Hartopp, Lord Mayor in 1697, took down John Owen's sermons in shorthand, learnt Hebrew at 50, and expected high theological discussion each Sunday in his family.

Those two pictures of Dissent, Dr Nuttall's and that which Isaac Watts encountered, complement each other. The progress from one to the other passes through a persecution which the wealthy survived with impunity and which men of the eminence of John Owen were almost able to ignore. The judgements that ensue are inevitable.

First: there were, by 1700, two clear strata in Dissent: that on the one hand which emerged at Mark Lane, and that on the other which continued in the country villages. The disabilities that were left with Dissenters after 1690 were oppressive to the poor among them, and it was for the mighty among them to look for their redress. Not all Dissent was violently persecuted between 1662 and 1689; those who could buy themselves out of trouble cheerfully did so, and it was the weakness of the legislation of those days that left this loophole to the wealthy. Had it not been left, there might have been none to harry the Establishment in the manner we are about to describe.

Second: that separatist Freedom, Fellowship and Holiness which were the nerve of classic Dissent underwent certain important changes once Dissent emerged from oppression. It was no longer necessary, as a principle of survival, for Dissenters to know one another intimately (and thus to be able to recognize spies), to cultivate an ascetic way that would stand them in good stead when they suffered, and to insist on a freedom from external secular allegiances which had now been granted to them. What happened was the development of a pattern reformed by an intellectual emphasis that had never been absent from Dissent, but which now tended to draw all the other forces towards itself.

G. K. Chesterton, in his book on Bernard Shaw, wrote this about the Puritans:

> I should roughly define the first spirit in Puritanism thus. It was a refusal to contemplate God or goodness with anything lighter or milder than the most fierce concentration of the intellect. A Puritan originally meant a man whose mind had no holidays. To use his own favourite phrase, he would let no living thing come between him and his God; an attitude which involved eternal torture for him and a cruel contempt for all living things. It was better to worship in a barn than in a cathedral for the specific and specified reason that the cathedral was beautiful.[3]

'Roughly', we have to contend, is right. Chesterton, whose knowledge of Dissenting history was negligible, and whose appreciation of Dissenting religious values was extinguished by a nonconformist background, is there describing very happily that decadent Puritanism which we are about to encounter; but he says nothing there to the purpose about the 'Visible Saints' of the great days. His error is to attribute to them no passion, no active principle.

But Mark Lane is what Chesterton was looking for: a congregation of men and women to whom worship was primarily hearing sermons, who noted sermons down in shorthand, and who expected their minds to be exercised by the preacher but asked for little more. Dissenting worship in Watts's time normally consisted of two sung psalms, two periods of prayer, a reading of Scripture and an extensive sermon, which was often detached as a separate act from the strict exposition of the Scriptures. This might well occupy the better part of two hours. Strickland Gough in his *Enquiry into the Decay of the Dissenting Interest* (1730) observed that 'to worship God for 20 minutes and to dictate to men for 60, is not so equal as one could wish', and justice was with him.

There was a real danger that this intellectualism would altogether kill the imagination. It is a wonder that it did not kill it in Watts himself; but (Chesterton could hardly be expected to have noticed this) perhaps the greatest imaginative literature of Puritanism is to be found in the best of Watts's hymns, where, with perseverance in thrusting through the doggerel and bathos, you can encounter such couplets as

> The voice that rolls the stars along
>   Speaks all the promises,
>
> Where reason fails with all her powers,
> There faith prevails, and love adores.

2. Dissenting academies

But intellectualism, in a pejorative sense, is to be distinguished from the love of learning; and at their best the Puritans were eminent in this. Under the Corporation and Test Acts Dissenters were firmly excluded from the existing English universities (Oxford, Cambridge and Durham). But it at once seemed good to the ministers of Dissent that they should personally provide opportunity for young men to educate themselves to the standard required by the universities, and to a standard which the ministry, should they be called to enter it, had a right to require of them. Thus, within a year of the Ejection, the long tradition of Dissenting academies was begun: a minister in Coventry, John Bryan, gathered a few students in his own house in 1663, and the practice was copied in other places where Dissenters continued to preach. When the minister was ejected, so far as possible, he would take his 'academy' with him; when he died, it usually died as well unless his successor took it over. After Toleration it became possible for the academies to expand, for assistant tutors to be provided, and for more pupils to be attracted and trained. And as the eighteenth century proceeded, the academies expanded, extending their curricula to include subjects far beyond the range of the universities, offering business training as well as literary education, and often run by boards of directors who engaged their staffs for full-time teaching. A Dissenting academy organized and managed by Philip Doddridge (1702–51) of Northampton, and another founded in 1730 at Newington Green, near London, are the direct ancestors of New College, London, which is now a college recognized in the University of London, primarily engaged in the training of Congregational ministers; while the famous Warrington Academy (founded 1757) survives in Manchester College, Oxford, and the Carmarthen Academy, dating back as far as 1700, had an unbroken existence until, in 1959, it was merged with another college and transferred to Swansea.

These academies became centres of liberal education providing a more extensive and far-flung training than the universities, clericalized and classicized as they were, could hope to offer. They were the direct consequence of that same love of learning which had caused the Pilgrim Fathers to found Harvard University for the perpetuation of a high scholarly tradition in the New World.[4]

That was Puritan intellectual culture at its best. At its worst, it led Dissent into a slough from which it could be rescued only by the genius of John Wesley. The theological controversies concerning Predestination and the Doctrine of the Trinity that occupied the time of all the most distinguished Dissenters from the Salter's Hall controversy of 1719 onwards provide some of the most barren pages of church history, and it is pleasant to be able with a good conscience, since this is not a book for theologians, to pass lightly over them here. It is, however, of importance to make clear that it was out of these controversies that the modern form of Unitarianism emerged.

3. *Rationalism and Deism*

As we move into the eighteenth century we move into the most urbane of English ages, and the spiritual coefficient of that urbanity is Deism. As Basil Willey so admirably put it: 'So beneficently had God planned the world, that by giving full rein to his acquisitive appetites the individual was, in fact, adding his maximum quota to the sum of human happiness.'[5] We have, indeed, moved out of the age in which, to the prevailing religious temper, 'nature' was prima facie corrupt into that in which it was prima facie good. Professor Willey sums it all up decisively in a classic chapter where he bids us contrast the medieval system, where the Law of Nature was a primary check on exuberant individualism or on wrongdoing, with the seventeenth century, where Nature was something from whose bondage man must escape; and both with the eighteenth century, where nature was something with which man at his best strives to conform. This he calls 'Cosmic Toryism', and directs our attention to the difference between the notion of 'romance', or the hidden good, in Dante, where it is out of this world yet seen in the categories of sense and sensual order; in the *Pilgrim's Progress*, where it is seen as the result of discipline and as a strictly heavenly reward; and in *Robinson Crusoe*, where it is frankly a natural conquest.

Deism goes with Cosmic Toryism because if your new discovery is that you can accept the universe—and if the reader will refresh his memory by reading a page or two of Calvin or Baxter he will remind himself how new a discovery this was—then you protest at once against the religious paradoxes of the Incarnation and the Atonement. You become aware that evil is not, as your fathers thought, something which God alone can conquer, but that it is a blemish on a fair creation which social reforms will put right. You turn your back on religious enthusiasm, on the miraculous, on a high doctrine of Revelation, because all these things imply disparagement of man and creation. You exalt the natural conscience, the advance of enlightenment, the pursuit of social order. The 'natural' is not now the 'primitive' or the 'bestial', but rather the 'civilized'.

Now any ultra-evangelical indignation at this development is not only out of place in these pages but is, absolutely considered, an affectation. Out of Deism came several things that the country greatly needed at the time. Deism was a protest against some of the things against which Wesley protested (though Wesley hated Deism like the plague). But when the minds of certain Dissenting leaders turned to these things, to the great humane advance represented by Toleration, to the new prosperity of the country and the new enterprise of the neo-Puritan British, to the revival of artistic culture and the exciting prospect of so much that was new, they heard from past history a note that chimed sympathetically with their furtive questions about their religion. Had there not been a pair of foreigners—Italians by descent—who had protested in Poland against Calvinist reformed doctrines, who had rejected the classic theory of the Atonement, and had extolled reason, virtuous living and social righteousness? Why yes—Fausto Sozzini (1539–1604), commonly called Socinus, and his uncle Lelio (1526–62)—those were the men, and their doctrine had been developed in the Rako-vian Catechism. They had been cast out as heretics, of course, and another who had made similar suggestions in Calvin's hearing, Servetus, was burnt in Geneva in 1552. But was there not something to be salvaged from this?

John Biddle (1615–62), Master of Gloucester Grammar School, had thought so, and had been imprisoned three times between 1644 and 1662 by the Puritans. Thomas Firmin (1632–97) had taken the same line—and, signi-ficantly, had become a pioneer of prison reform. And the Presbyterians, it was suddenly found, were beginning to take the notion of Deism, with the associated doctrine of Unitarianism, quite seriously. The Dean of St Paul's, William Sherlock (1641–1707), attacked these views, and was (surprisingly) rebuked by the Convocation of Oxford University, who had been irritated by a sermon from one of his disciples, for being a 'tritheist'. In 1697 an Act of Parliament made disbelief in the Blessed Trinity a penal offence. Clearly the landslide was beginning.

In the controversies that gathered round the trial of three West-country Presbyterian ministers for heresy in 1719 the most significant and familiar-looking figure is William Whiston. He was not involved in the contro-versies, he was not a Dissenting minister: he was a Pro-fessor of Mathematics at Cambridge. That implied that he was in Anglican orders, but in his writings he manifests a neo-scientific scepticism that would have appealed to readers of religious journalism of the nineteen-twenties.[6] Whiston was a defender of 'the primitive' in doctrine, as much as the best of Puritans a century before had been, but he advocated a rationalism that inspired many of the early Deists.

In the end, although it was an Anglican clergyman who

had made the running, Dissent was very largely influenced by Unitarianism; and the reason why the Presbyterians of England embraced it so much more hospitably than did the Independents and Baptists can only be answered speculatively. It is perhaps not too hazardous to suggest that the Presbyterian Dissenter was on the whole likely to be a somewhat more intellectually developed and less evangelically simple person than the Independent or the Baptist. At all events, English Presbyterianism gave itself very largely to Unitarianism and from the second quarter of the eighteenth century to the present time the Unitarians —who a generation ago were more numerous than they are at present—formed among Dissenters an intellectual aristocracy comparable with the philanthropic aristocracy of the Quakers. It is for this reason that the Presbyterian Church of England remains a denomination much smaller than the Congregational Union.

In the course of the Deistic controversy there was a quantity of personal mud-slinging and witch-hunting which consorted ill with the Cosmic Toryism that made Deism so 'chearful' (to use its favourite adjective). That aspect of it was extremely disedifying; but it must be admitted that on the whole the controversy was urban, and the idolatry of the intellect also was urban. The less agreeable aspects of Puritanism are mostly attributable in the last resort to the dangerously close relation that existed historically between Puritan culture and the divorce of Englishmen from nature and the soil. Deism in particular goes historically with the 'urbane' architecture of an eighteenth-century terrace or manor house. Outwardly, it is incomparably symmetrical and rational. What happens within is no concern of him who looks on from without. And what happened in the villages of Staffordshire, and that Cornish country which was commonly called 'West Barbary', when Wesley first set eyes on them, was of very little interest to the philosophers and debaters of Deism.

4. *The Meeting House*

Rustic Dissent, largely spared these complexities, but lacking also the prestige and power of its urban counterpart, began to establish itself as a domestic bourgeois religious habit. Rustic Anglicanism grew more and more aristocratic: those who were neither bourgeois nor aristocrats, the remnant of the medieval villeins, were left to Wesley to evangelize. But for what it was worth, Dissent in the market towns and villages became part of the normal scenery. Its domestic *ethos* is best seen by examining any one of the few genuine early eighteenth century meeting-houses that now remain standing. Note the name—'meeting-house'. That, not 'chapel', is the historic name for a Dissenting place of worship. The implication is not merely that they met each other there, but that they met the Lord; it is a fairly precise translation of the Greek word 'synagogue', and its worship corresponded, with its emphasis on word rather than on sacrament and symbol, with what took place in the synagogues of the Old and New Testaments.

It was, and looked like, a 'house' rather than a church. Its architecture was always domestic and functional, rather than ceremonious or symbolic. It was given an address, but not usually a 'Christian name'. Not then (though fairly often now) 'St John's' or 'St Luke's', but simply 'Swanland Meeting', or, if it were in a large city, 'Mark Lane Meeting', 'Jewin Street Meeting'. This was not (*pace* Chesterton) a deliberate cult of the prosaic, but a natural

expression of the domesticities of worship. The idea of its
ever becoming the parish church had, as we have said,
gone. It was where people went who knew each other and
formed a Christian family. 'Family' was a favourite
Puritan word—family worship, family prayers, family
loyalty (even when it became, in New England, the Dear
Octopus kind of loyalty), and family simplicity were there.

In the longer side of the rectangular interior there would
be a commodious pulpit, placed there so that none of
those who sat in church would be far from the preacher.
They sat most of the time: they sat, as for a lecture, while
the long sermon was preached: they sat with bowed heads
for prayer. Sometimes, but not always, they stood to sing.
They were silent except when they sang. They made no
audible response to prayer. They often regarded even the
repetition of the Lord's Prayer as a 'rag of popery',
preferring that the minister pray *ex tempore*, moulding his
utterance on the words and phrase and thought-forms of
the King James Bible. Eloquence was expected inside the
church, but the building and its furnishings were not
themselves eloquent. What such things would have had to
say everybody present knew, and a new member would not
be admitted until he had been carefully instructed in the
Faith and in the principles of Dissent. The idea of an
unchurched mass to whom the very building and its
furnishing should appeal was never more utterly absent
from orthodox Dissent than it was from the meeting-house
of about 1730. The communion table, in front of the pulpit,
was used perhaps four times a year, and when in use it was
furnished with a plate and cup of good but not pretentious
workmanship, and in a simple liturgy the members, seated
in their places, would serve each other as the plate and the
cup passed from hand to hand. Devotion and good works

11   John Wesley

12 Swanland Independent Chapel

abounded within the congregation, rectitude and honour usually adorned their lives; and if any member transgressed, there were the elders and the minister, whom they knew well, to reason with them. Excommunication was used when a member showed no sign of consciousness that he had done wrong; dishonesty in business was especially frowned on, and bankruptcy, deemed to be a sign of dishonesty and therefore of gross failure in neighbourly discipline, was the commonest ground for excommunication.

5. *The Evangelical Revival and Methodism*

That was the best, and Salter's Hall the worst, of what John Wesley found at the moment when he was moved to evangelize the country. The Methodist Church, which is now in England the most powerful non-Anglican influence and must be reckoned as part of organized Dissent, was (as everybody knows) the consequence of the movement of inspiration in two Anglican priests of curious and remarkable gifts.

The story of Methodism may be read fully in all manner of books. Methodism was perhaps the most significant and violent of all the Dissents that invaded English religion. For the Wesleys, though not formally dissenting from the Church of England, dissented against almost everything else that they saw in English religious life. Put succinctly, the Wesleyan dissent was in the first place against Calvinism, eighteenth-century style, against Deism, and against the outrageous social injustices and corruptions that were increasingly disfiguring English society.

It did not, perhaps, present itself to John Wesley in just those terms all at once. At Oxford, as a Fellow of Lincoln

College, with his younger brother at Christ Church, the accent for John Wesley was on holiness. With certain other pious souls, the Wesleys founded the 'Holy Club', in order to practise a strict devotional life and to help the poor. Dissatisfied, as any healthy-minded person was bound to be after a few years of this, John Wesley looked about him. *Robinson Crusoe* had been published a few years before, but there is no evidence that he read it. None the less, his desire to move significantly into the prevailing religious apathy of the surrounding world took the strictly romantic form of a project to found, on the lines that the Pilgrim Fathers had followed, a new state of saints in Georgia, U.S.A. First and last the relative failure of this enterprise (and we must remember that our judgement that it was a failure rests almost entirely on Wesley's own estimate of it recorded in his Journal) was probably due to the incomplete integration of his religious convictions with his consciousness of the world's need. The experiences he had in Georgia, anyhow, were such as to wash away fairly quickly any sediment of romanticism that lay over his missionary convictions. But in the course of this project the Wesleys came into close contact with certain German pietists who were themselves seeking a revival of religion in their own country by going again over the ground that had been travelled three centuries before by John Hus. In Moravian pietism, which is the name given to the cult of those who so profoundly influenced the Wesleys at this point, we have a revival of that German Lollardy which sent men back to their Bibles and their prayers, and sent them out to work acts of charity for their less fortunate neighbours. Here was what Wesley was looking for—efficient and significant action backed by a system of piety whose essential simplicity anybody could grasp.

146

Seeing this, Wesley realized perhaps for the first time what it was that he must fight in England. It was his own Puritan inheritance that had to so large an extent held him back. If the Moravians were right, then certain things followed. One must not propagate a religion that only the intellectually mature could grasp: that was the mistake of the Presbyterians and Independents. One must not propagate and insist on a church order that excluded all but the reasonably holy: another Puritan error. One must not preach a gospel that frightened people out of their wits when one's audience was *ex hypothesi* made up of people who were already sufficiently terrified by the power of disease, poverty and beastliness: that was a Calvinist error, and for it must be substituted a message that left 'salvation' open to any who would profess the need for it. One must not—good heavens! one must not—adopt habits of worship and church life that suggested that all was right with the world, and that a little common sense and co-operation all round would make that evident. What good was that to the wives of drink-sodden husbands in Gornal and Redruth? Finally, it was no use waiting until these people came into church: they must be met where they stood, in the open air or anywhere else that might be convenient.

That is surely part of the intellectual content of Wesley's 'conversion' of 1738.[7] The fusion of all these notions with a certain emotional drive whose components are familiarly noted in the Journal, caused that 'warming of the heart' which sent Wesley invincibly to the corners of England.[8]

This was a revival, at the moment when Puritanism was sinking into a reasonably comfortable doze, of the very essence of primitive Puritanism. It was, you might almost say, the new Lollardy. The social state of England was hardly less grievous in Wesley's time than it was in Wyclif's.

A formidably large number of people, in both ages, were in ignorance of the Gospel, though the ignorance was deeper in Wesley's day because of the removal even of the symbolic outer structure of religion that Catholic Europe had preserved. And so Wesley began an adventure which forces from the historian the judgement that he was the most successful religious revivalist who ever breathed. He lived to be eighty-seven, and before his death he could look out on England and see every major contention of his fifty-year-old ambitions accepted and acted upon. Other reformers have lived long and seen much less; others achieved much but died in the belief that they had achieved little or nothing. But Wesley really did live to see it. He saw the revival of social consciousness in the foundation of a string of orphanages, charity schools, and asylums; the revival of concern for the young in the foundation of Sunday schools; the popularizing of religion through a massive organization of chapels, classes and circuits; the very invention of the technique of the lay-preacher; the invention of a new religious technique in the popular hymn;[9] the very revival of religion in remote places where there had been none before but superstition; the revival of a concern in Christians that others should hear the Gospel; the devotion of one man after another to works of charity and social rehabilitation among the prisoners, the destitute, and even the insane. All he did not live to see—and he missed it by only one year—was the foundation of the first of the Dissenting Missionary Societies (the Baptist) in 1792.

Now a closely argued history of the eighteenth century would require modification of some of these generalities. It might, were we engaged on such a work, be our business to assess how much of the social reform of these generations and of the religious revival would have taken place had there been no Wesley. Even here we must insist that a great deal of the post-Wesleyan revival of social consciousness was due to people with whom Wesley had no direct contact. But, however far we might have gone into it, we should have been left with this conclusion in the end: that Wesley made of his revival in England and Wales a force that nobody in either country could ignore. Even those who most disagreed with him were influenced by him. With a fine judgement which even an historian must ascribe in part to the Holy Spirit if he be a Christian (to chance and contingency if he be not), Wesley injected into English religion the precise combination of warmth, enthusiasm, personal involvement, realism, hospitality and social common sense that it needed after a century and a half of learned orthodoxy opposed by learned Lollardy. Now and again the mixture, one part unduly disproportioned, turned either explosive or merely sour. Reaction against Puritan austerities could produce irresponsibility; reaction against Puritan fastidiousness could bring in the thief and the robber; reaction against Puritan psalm-singing could bring the encouragement of musical ranting; and the success-story could and did bring a host of secondary persons who looked for a place on the bandwagon. John Wesley himself remained stern and critical; the older he grew the more monkishly observant of tendencies to spiritual decay or excess he became. But compared with the real and abiding success of what he achieved, the early persecutions of Wesley, the stonings in the Black Country and the frowns of the conventional clergy who eventually inhibited him from ministering in their parishes were as nothing.

The precise date at which Methodism became a separate denomination is difficult to determine. In a perfectly legitimate sense, Methodists can claim that their society was founded in 1739 when Wesley's evangelical campaigns began. The word 'Methodists' is itself of obscure origin, but John Wesley gave it a special sense as early as 1729 when he applied it to those who followed the strict 'method' or rule of life associated with the Holy Club at Oxford. It was not until 1784 that, by ordaining two presbyters to assist one Thomas Coke who had been set aside as superintendent of a mission in America, John Wesley provoked an open breach with the Church of England, although from 1760 he had approved the setting-apart of lay evangelists who had the right to administer the sacraments within their societies. In 1784 also he made provision for an annual 'Conference' by nominating 100 persons who were deemed to be members of that conference, and prescribing principles by which their successors might be appointed. This was virtually the outward establishment of the denomination, for it indicates John Wesley's despair of ever persuading the Church of England to regard the Methodists as an 'order' within their communion. In later years certain separations occurred within Methodism: of the Primitive Methodists in 1810 under Hugh Bourne, of the Bible Christians in 1815 under William O'Bryan, of the Wesleyan Methodist Association and the Wesleyan Reformers who joined to become the United Methodists in 1857; apart from a few dissidents, the Methodist Connexion was reunited in 1932.

If anything can be added to our estimate of Wesley as the major force in the revival of English religion in the eighteenth century, it must needs be by way of saying that the fire that burnt in Wesley burnt also in others who did not know him and were not directly under his influence. It would be ludicrous to claim that the Wesleys alone of the population of England saw the necessity for revival, or to undervalue the local work of pious and inspired preachers of every denomination—Benjamin Beddome the Independent, Daniel Turner and Andrew Fuller, Baptists, and above all Philip Doddridge, the first of the Independents to urge consistently on his people and his pupils the necessity of missionary work.[10] But it was the Wesleys who focused it, and then disseminated it. And here perhaps was the secret of all this 'success', that so many clergy of the Church of England were infected with the 'Evangelical' spirit. The consequence of this was a real breaking down of local barriers between clergy of this mind and Dissenters. An excellent example is the co-operation, which would do justice to the most ecumenically minded modern parish, between the Baptist minister, Sutcliff, and the curate, John Newton, at Olney, Buckinghamshire, in the years 1775–9. Such happy events were not widespread, for many bishops caused clergy of the 'evangelical' mind to be deprived of their licences, and frequently the village parson was the very reverse of 'evangelical' in his habits. But in as much as Wesley, from his peculiar position half in and half out of the Church of England, affected indifferently many people on either side of the line of Dissent, the contribution of Methodism to the reconciliation of the Churches was probably larger in its first years than it has ever been since. At all events, through this influence on many parishes, the 'evangelical' spirit touched men and women who proceeded in the next century to apply it to the social problems and grievances of their time with consequences for which all their posterity has cause to thank them.

The Quakers and the Rationalist Dissenters had little to do with the Evangelical Revival: the reasons are not far to seek. The Quakers were already eminent in their advocacy and practice of social righteousness, while the Rationalist Dissenters were turning their minds habitually in a different direction. Not that we should undervalue the significance of Rationalist Dissent when it throws up a man of the stature of Joseph Priestley (1733–1804). Priestley was one of the first of those scientist-ministers who in our own time have become a familiar and valuable part of church life. He was a practising chemist of some eminence, and along with it, a rationalist, inquiring, sceptical Christian. Naturally, in that day, he was of the Unitarian-Presbyterian persuasion; but he was a pioneer in the field of Christian rational inquiry which became a century later the special preserve of German and English Protestant theologians.

But an account of the missionary and political work of Dissent in the early nineteenth century must wait until we have briefly examined the history of that orthodox Dissent with which Wesley was so discontented. This can be most serviceably done by offering some account of the work of the Dissenting Deputies.[11]

6. *The Dissenting Deputies*

It is very much to the credit of the farthest-seeing among the Dissenters of 1689 that they recognized at once the fact that, once Toleration even of this limited sort was achieved, they must do what they could to reduce unnecessary multiplication of denominations within Dissent to a minimum. The outstanding differences within Dissent are simply marked by divisions in two planes. On the one hand there was the difference of opinion between those who believed in infant baptism and those who believed in adult baptism. This, though there had been discussions, turned out to be an intractable problem; and indeed it has remained so. The other division was that which had formed itself in 1644 between the Presbyterians and the Independents. This controversy, not yet half a century old, certain divines of both parties set themselves to consider and, if possible, to heal, in the year 1690. To this end these ministers compiled and published a document entitled *Heads of Agreement assented to by the United Ministers in and about London formerly called Presbyterian and Congregational.* Between eighty and ninety ministers entered into this agreement, one of whose provisions was that the denominational names should be dropped on both sides, and that they should thenceforward be known as the 'United Brethren'. This gesture towards a United Free Church of England came to grief early for two highly suggestive reasons. The occasion of the rupture was a criticism directed by the United Brethren at the teaching of a minister in the country—one Mr Davis of Rothwell, Northamptonshire. The justice of the criticism need not be in question, but immediately the criticism was objected to, and the limitations of the United Brethren became apparent; for the real reasons why the union could not be more significant and persuasive were first that it was primarily a London union, and second that it was entirely a clerical union. Time and again in the subsequent history of Dissent we find high-minded attempts at rational church policy frustrated because those who promote them forget the importance of the layman, and the Englishman's suspicion of centralization. London might not dictate to the provinces beyond a certain point; nor, in Dissent, was it ever wise for the ministers to ignore the laity for long.

But despite its early failure, this union between the two denominations did indicate that some saw a difference between denominational interests and 'the Dissenting interest'. They were united in the demands they wished to make of society and in the disabilities they suffered. Therefore movements towards a limited kind of union were naturally to be made.

What precisely were these disabilities? Here are some examples. Up to the year 1753 marriages in Dissenting meeting-houses were often held to be invalid: from 1753 to 1836 the law made it clear that they were always invalid. In 1747 a Dissenter who was married in the meeting-house at Fairford, Gloucestershire, was arrested for fornication. Baptisms in such meeting-houses were often declared invalid, although here, since no legal contract is involved, the judgement was a theological one and had no substance in law. Up to 1900, burial in parish churchyards was denied to Dissenters. The universities were closed to them: and the first university, that of London, to be open to them was founded largely in order that they might circumvent the tradition which in respect of Oxford, Cambridge and Durham persisted until 1871.

These were the most evident of the disabilities under which Dissenters lay after Toleration, and there were always Dissenters bold enough to make their grievances known. But how were they to evolve a technique by which they could speak to the State and to the State Church with one voice, and impressively? The State had its capital in London, and the London people were the most likely to be able to have access to them. Ministers were, it was thought, more likely to be able to voice the opinions of their churches. Three Dissenting ministers had presented a loyal address to Queen Anne on her accession; a larger number (as we saw) presented one to George I at his; gestures of loyalty could well be followed up by gestures of respectful demand. So the 'General Board' of Dissenting ministers in London was formed in 1727, with the object of working systematically for the redress of grievances. But this ran into the same troubles. Once any controversial business came up, the laymen would not be dictated to by the ministers, nor the country by the capital.

It was, then, in 1732 that the Board of Dissenting Deputies was formed; and it was formed entirely of laymen. Two members were to be annually chosen from each of the Three Denominations (as they were widely known), Congregationalist, Presbyterian and Baptist, from churches within twelve miles of the city of London. From these a committee of twenty-one was selected for executive duties, whose Secretary was always a lawyer.

The first business of the Deputies was to urge the repeal of the Test Act. Walpole, interviewed in 1735, was courteous but non-committal. 'No, the Test Act could not conveniently be repealed at this juncture; after all (as the learned Deputies would agree), we must not open the door to the Catholics' (an argument they had heard before but had not yet the courage to circumvent or rebut). Walpole granted a handsome donation from public funds for the relief of distressed Dissenters. The Deputies went away and conducted quiet propaganda in the country districts. ('No, we are not clergy, and we respect the views of the villages. Now help us!') Another attempt on the Test Act was made in 1739, and this time Walpole was rather less expansive. Parliament would never permit it. Please drop the subject.

The Deputies then addressed themselves to other items on the agenda. Specific cases of distress and injustice were collected, and as their power became known in the villages, the villages sent in fuller and more frequent reports. There were cases of illegal impressment into the forces in 1745.

Local rate-collectors were liable to 'take their pen and write fifty' where Dissenting ratepayers were concerned. Tolls remitted to churchgoers were collected from chapel-goers. In 1838 there was a case where a group of Welsh tenants who voted against their landlord's Tory interests in Parliament (they had lively memories of the smelting furnaces in north-east Glamorgan) were evicted from their cottages: the Deputies paid £21 for their relief. In 1811 certain schoolboys at Harrow school threw stones at the local Baptist minister and his congregation, and broke the chapel windows and damaged their conveyances. The Deputies remonstrated with Dr Butler, the headmaster, claiming damages for the sake of the Baptist minister and his people. They received an apology, and paid for the damage themselves. The 'church–chapel' mind in villages and country towns might at any time give rise to a riot in which property was damaged: the Deputies would be told, and would go to law, and if the law gave no relief, they would themselves provide what they could. In an age when the sovereign counted for less and Parliament for more in the forming of public opinion, a change of government might bring a change of climate for Dissenters. In the seventeen-fifties opinion moved sharply against them, because of the contentions of certain exalted Tories; and there was one case, known as the 'Sherriff's cause', which the Deputies fought for twenty-five years, from 1742 to 1767. It was a revival of the technique of appointing a known Dissenter to public office and then fining him for failing to accept it. Robert Grosvenor was appointed Sheriff of the City of London in 1742, and on declining the office because of the requirements of the Test Act, he was prosecuted for the sum of £620. This was the beginning of a series of such cases. The Deputies raised a guarantee fund of £4000, largely from presents given to them by those whom they had successfully defended. And they fought the case on principle. They eventually won it in 1767, by which time the original parties on their side were dead or dying.

The repeal of the Five Mile Act and the Conventicle Act, which were all this time on the Statute-book, came by the Deputies' efforts in 1811, and that of the Test and Corporation Acts in 1828.

After this happy consummation of their hopes—ninety-six years after the Test Act had first appeared on their agenda, the Deputies turned their attention to Disestablishment, and later to the matter of education. These affairs belong to a later chapter; it is enough here to say that the Dissenting Deputies are still in existence as a constituted body, although at this present time they are rarely called on to perform more than merely formal duties. But their importance in the history of Dissent is enormous. They were the first and most eminent of all Dissenting laymen's movements. By their efficiency and energy they succeeded in making known to the country at large the substance and the potency of the Dissenting interest. And by perseverance they achieved what they set out to achieve: the removal of one disability after another. Among the prominent people who were of their number were Sir Samuel Morton Peto (1809–89), architect and designer of the Nelson Column in London, Sir Charles Reed, M.P. (1819–81), founder of the City of London Library, Samuel Morley, M.P. (1809–86), founder of Morley College, together with several Lord Mayors and Sheriffs of London and many prominent politicians including 'Liberty' Wilks (John Wilks, M.P. for Boston). The University of London owed its foundation principally to the activity of the Deputies.

CHAPTER IX

PROSPERITY, 1789–1892

1. *Rebellion and Romance*

The Dissenting Deputies, then, had seen to it that English Dissent became a permanent part of the national scene; and John Wesley had seen to it that at a time when many of its primitive contentions were being answered by the natural processes of history, it had something new to live for, namely, Evangelism. Now, as we approach the end of the eighteenth century, we must add something of greater importance than either of those two facts, which is, of course, the revolution of thought and culture that overtook the whole of Western Europe about that time. It is a revolution of which the French Revolution was one phase, the Industrial Revolution another, the 'Enlightenment' a third. Once again we have to place our story in a context, not of that national development with which we have been preoccupied in our account of the two and a half centuries, 1532–1789, but of that continental development which was the context of our opening chapters.

This movement, or development, or revolution—which was it?—has no official historians' name. It is, quite clearly, the 'far end' of the Renaissance. It is not merely the consequence of that interest in science and that recovery of philosophy which are the notable developments of the previous century and a half; it is not quite the 'recovery' of anything in the sense in which the Renaissance is the 'recovery' of learning. Its most obvious feature is what C. S. Lewis has called the 'unchristening' of Europe;[1] and in the lecture in which Professor Lewis made that judge-

158

ment there is a profound analysis of the symptoms that lead him to insist that somewhere about the turn of the nineteenth century there exists in history a 'great divide'. Whatever this ought to be called—and I must ask my reader either to take for granted the arguments for its existence or to read Professor Lewis's *De Descriptione Temporum* alongside the historical analysis in Paul Tillich's *The Courage to Be*—we can be quite sure, when examining the history of religious thought from about the time of the French Revolution onwards, that an entirely new wind was beginning to blow.

Consider, then, this passage from William Blake's Preface to *Milton*; consider not only the new tone it is taking with the whole of eighteenth-century 'urbanity', but the notes in it which chime with the millenarianism of the medieval enthusiasts.

The stolen and perverted writings of Homer and Ovid, of Plato and Cicero, which all men ought to contemn, are set up by artifice against the sublime of the Bible; but when the New Age is at leisure to pronounce, all will be set right, & those grand works of the more ancient & consciously & professedly Inspired Men will hold their proper rank, & the Daughters of Memory shall become the Daughters of Inspiration. Shakespeare and Milton were both curb'd by the general malady & infection from the silly Greek & Latin slaves of the Sword.

Rouze up, O Young Men of the New Age! set your foreheads against the ignorant hirelings! For we have hirelings in the camp, the court & the University, who would, if they could, for ever depress Mental and prolong Corporeal War. Painters! on you I call. Sculptors! Architects! Suffer not the fashionable fools to depress your powers by the prices they pretend to give for contemptible works, or the expensive advertizing boasts that they make of such works; believe Christ and his Apostles that there is a class of man whose whole delight is in destroying. We do not want either Greek or Roman Models if we are but just and true to our own Imaginations, those worlds in which we shall live for ever in JESUS OUR LORD.

And did those feet in ancient time
    Walk upon England's mountains green,
And was the holy Lamb of God
    In England's pleasant pastures seen?
And did the countenance divine
    Shine forth upon our clouded hills,
And was Jerusalem builded here,
    Among those dark satanic mills?

Bring me my bow of burning gold,
    Bring me my arrows of desire,
Bring me my spear, O clouds unfold!
    Bring me my chariot of fire.
I will not cease from mental fight
    Nor shall my sword sleep in my hand,
Till we have built Jerusalem
    In England's green and pleasant land.

Would to God that all the Lord's people were prophets!

If anybody would understand nineteenth-century Dissent, he must recognize that what was expressed in that paragraph, and what lay within those verses which, uncontexted, have become especially familiar among folk with whom Blake would have had little patience, represented something which was happening throughout Western Europe. Written in 1804, they focus and project, prophetwise, the largely unexpressed thoughts of that generation. Observe the fierce rebellion against the 'artificial', the appeal to 'Men of the New Age', the exaltation of the Hebrew mind of the Bible over the Greek-and-Latin mind of the Renaissance; observe the call to the artist to insist on his integrity, and to believe that in so doing he has Christ with him; observe the hatred of 'corporeal war' and the insistence on 'mental fight'. 'The Classics!', wrote Blake at another point,[2] 'it is the Classics, and not Goths nor Monks, that desolate Europe with wars.' 'Christianity is Art and not Money. Money is a curse!'[3] And, for our

13   The Mission Station at Inyati, 1860

14 Westminster Chapel (Congregational)

own purposes, with startling relevance, 'All the Destruction in Christian Europe has arisen from Deism, which is Natural Religion'.[4]

Here is violent revolt against typically eighteenth-century values—urbanity, commerce, optimism, natural religion. It might seem to have little to do with the history of Dissent, which prospered so spectacularly in its practice of those values; but, on the contrary, it alone explains the paradoxes and contradictions in Dissent, and in all English religion, which show themselves in the age of the industrial revolution. For every man born after 1800 in England was a child of the Romantic movement, even as every man born after 1500 was a child of the Renaissance: and the Romantic movement is not a babbling of green fields, but, more essentially, the wrath of Blake.

Romance, says Professor C. S. Lewis,[5] includes among other things a spirit of adventure, a subjective emphasis, a cult of the marvellous and the titanic, a revolt against artificiality, a naturalism, and a sense of longing for a mysterious object. All this is in Blake; and it is in the air. The collision between the disciplined practicality of the eighteenth century and this kind of vision is what gives us the clue to the nineteenth century. To my own mind one of the most revealing documents of religious romanticism, coming this time not from that arch-Dissenter, Blake, but from the very centre of organized and respectable religious Dissent, is a hymn by Thomas Binney, a leader of Congregationalism who ministered in London from 1829 to 1874, which contains these lines—

> Eternal Light! Eternal Light!
>   How pure the soul must be
> When placed within thy searching sight
> It shrinks not, but with calm delight
>   Can live, and look on Thee....

> O how shall I, whose native sphere
>   Is dark, whose mind is dim,
> Before the Ineffable appear
> And on my naked spirit bear
>   The uncreated beam?

Awe and longing are there, a sense of poetry, almost a dwelling on the longing. It is a remarkable and revealing utterance for a Calvinist.

But romanticism touched Dissent chiefly at the point of 'adventure'. Dissent is still formally protesting against disabilities and the patronizing scorn of the Church of England. But the Evangelical Revival has added a touch of romance to life, and the new note of 'conquering new lands for Christ' in church life matches the commercial enterprise for which the century has already made itself famous.

2. *Missions*

Societies for foreign missionary work of the modern sort were by no means begun by Dissenters, for the Anglican Society for Promoting Christian Knowledge goes back to 1698, and the Society for the Propagation of the Gospel to 1701. But it was the liberation brought by the Evangelical Revival that stirred the Baptists to form the Baptist Missionary Society in 1792, upon hearing a sermon from William Carey (1761–1834) on 'the obligations of Christians to use means for the conversion of the Heathens'. More significant, perhaps, is the foundation of the London Missionary Society in 1795, for this was an interdenominational enterprise including evangelically-minded Anglicans (some of whom had been inhibited for their Methodist-like practices) as well as nonconformists. Here, typically, denominational differences were set aside in the cause of (in their phrase) 'preaching the glorious Gospel of the

Blessed God'. That society pledged itself to take the Gospel only, and not any particular form of church government, to the ends of the earth. Another inter-denominational missionary effort was the foundation in 1804 of the British and Foreign Bible Society. Methodist missionary societies began with the Wesleyan Missionary Society in 1813. The Scottish Missionary Society began unofficially in 1796, and the General Assembly of the Church of Scotland formed its Missionary Committee in 1824.

From these, in which Dissenters played so prominent a part, went out men of adventure and religious integrity under the conviction that the Christian faith must be preached to all the nations. Comparable efforts were made by continental Protestants. For something like 150 years the missionary effort of the English Protestants was a story of unchallenged heroism. It is only in these latest days that problems have arisen which fall outside the scope of our present story. But to take but one example, the united Church of South India, which includes ministers and congregations who in England would be held Dissenters alongside those in communion with the Church of England, is an example of the consequence of this non-denominational missionary effort; and the long and painful gestation that preceded the formation of that Church in 1947, and the controversy that continues around it, are likewise an indication of the perils of an Evangelical approach which sets aside historic denominational differences.

John Williams of the South Seas, Robert Morrison of China, Roger Price of Bechuanaland, and in our own generation Alfred Sadd of the Gilberts are among the many distinguished names in the story of Dissenting

missionary work, but none is more familiar than that of
David Livingstone (1813–73), who in the first place went
to Africa as a Congregationalist from Scotland. On the
one hand, in British enterprise, we have the zealous missionaries whose one idea is to evangelize the heathen: on
the other (and not necessarily, though inevitably sometimes, over against them) the colonizers and traders who
seek to extend the frontiers of the empire and to share the
benefits of Western civilization with the 'natives'. Livingstone stands midway between. Livingstone was a believing Christian of missionary spirit, but he was also a
naturalist and an explorer, and the story of his two visits to
Africa is worth pondering in relation to the larger context
of this study. On his first visit, 1841–57, he was a missionary of the London Missionary Society; on his second
and third, 1858–1864 and 1865–73, he was officially an
emissary of the British government, but to all practical
purposes a free-lance. In Livingstone, as the popularity
of books and films about him testifies, we have the supreme
adventurer-missionary, combining a missionary zeal of the
spirit with, on the one hand, a highly practical concern for
the physical privations of backward races and, on the
other, a dauntless and eager compulsion to explore.

The mission-field provided opportunity for all the
heroism and self-sacrifice to which religious men and
women in Britain felt called in this new age, and Dissenters
almost hand-in-hand with Anglicans offered themselves
freely and eagerly for such work. But at home the call to
adventure was hardly less, and parallel with the triumphant
missionary expansion of the nineteenth century we see
Dissenters involving themselves deeply in political and
social reform.

3. Politics

It was one of the great glories of the Rational Dissenters— Joseph Priestley in the lead, and with him, Robert Hall and Richard Price—that before the end of the eighteenth century they had carefully and emphatically defined the duty of Dissent to support and promote civil liberty. Those who were concerning themselves through their Deputies for their own rights were not too busy to insist on the rights of others. Priestley's *Address to Protestant Dissenters*, Hall's *Apology for the Freedom of the Press*, and Price's *Observations on the Nature of Civil Liberty*, all published before 1800, laid a good foundation for the prominent part which Dissenters took in the agitation towards the Reform Bill of 1832. Dissent was flourishing in those new cities which the Bill sought to enfranchise, and it was Dissenters, brought up to revere liberty and to profess liberal politics, who spoke loudest in defence of the reform.[6] There is, in R. G. Cowherd's *The Politics of English Dissent*, an interesting collocation of quotations from the reactions of Dissent to the Reform Act after it was passed. 'The Dissenters rejoiced in many places that "the long conflict with corruption is over". The Methodists felt that the "Reform Bill affords an opportunity for pious people to express themselves".' It was a combination of ancient Puritan rationalism with ancient Puritan social righteousness that was at work here, rather more than Evangelical piety.

The Dissenting support for the Reform Bill was but one aspect of the activities of a group of Evangelicals who formed themselves into a progressive group to work for social reform in 1804. They are usually referred to as 'The Clapham Sect', although that is a misuse of the word 'sect'. Their first leader was William Wilberforce, whose pioneer work for the abolition of slavery was accompanied by many other manifestations of a lively social conscience. It had been the Quakers who in the eighteenth century had protested much about this—as they had about the conditions in the prisons. It was given to Wilberforce to lead the movement which finally brought slavery to an end in English colonies; and this, perhaps, was a more strictly 'evangelical' activity than the political agitation associated with the Reform Bill. Wesley would have understood the liberation of human beings from bondage better, perhaps, than the reforming of the constitutional procedure of the realm. Wilberforce was, of course, not a Dissenter, but many of those associated with him were. The Clapham group, Bible-based and prayerful, was a notable manifestation of Puritanism within the Church of England, and a direct consequence of the Evangelical Revival.[7]

Dissenters played a prominent part in all the major social agitations of that time—the Anti Corn-Law League, the Ten Hours Bill, the agitation for State education, and Chartism. In these and similar activities they laid the foundations of that Liberal Party which later came to be especially identified with nonconformity.

An important by-product of this identification of Evangelicals, whether Dissenting, Anglican or Methodist, with movements of social reform was the cross-fertilization that ensued between Dissent and Methodism. Methodism was not of itself prone to social reform. It was concerned primarily with personal reform. It was seen by others than Methodists—Wilberforce, Shaftesbury, Bright, Cobden—to be a natural consequence of Evangelical Christianity that society should be reformed and grievances redressed; but when Methodists themselves became involved in social reform they naturally began to assimilate themselves to other Dissenting habits. It was this, more than anything else, that brought Methodism firmly down on the side of Dissent rather than on that of the Church of England, and caused Methodism to become the leading denomination of the Free Church Federal Council when that body was formed at the end of the century.

These are more mundane matters than the prophet Blake wanted to be concerned with, but the intellectual presuppositions were consequences of the same urge that produced Blake's angry prophecies. Blake hardly lived to see the machine-age transform England. His 'satanic mills' were mental and metaphysical—they are to be explained only by reference to the long poem that follows his Preface. But one of the things the Romantics said was, 'Let nature alone! Do not make it subservient to utility. Do not even make it subservient to theology!' Therefore it was necessary in the dark streets of the industrial cities for somebody to say, 'Let man alone, for man is the lord of nature'. And the emancipation of industrialized man was matter for all the heroism and adventure that a romantic could wish for.

Once Dissent had measured its strength in politics against the Establishment and Toryism, it remained closely involved in politics until the beginning of the twentieth century. By that time, Methodism was as ready as any other denomination to lift up its voice. The local chapels, with their local preachers, bred a race of articulate proletarians who were ready to bring ancient Puritan principles to bear on politics, and to found the Labour Party; the larger Churches with their intellectual and critical tradition produced a body of opinion that expressed itself finally in the Liberal government of 1906-10. If ever Dissent was an English Institution, is was so in that talented and progressive government. It may fairly be judged that the separation of the two broad classes of Dissent that produced Labour on the one hand and the Liberals on the other—a separation uncomfortably congruent with the class-separation that persisted in Victorian society—led to the decline alike of the prestige of Liberalism and of the power of nonconformity after 1914. But Liberalism still relies on intellectual Dissenters for its support, and numbers some of the most distinguished of them among its leaders. And at the present time it is the Liberal Party that lays most stress on the simple Puritan values in its political writings.[8]

4. *Prestige*

But it will be asked by now, what brought Dissent, still officially living under political disabilities, to this remarkable influence and prestige? Once again, a combination of romantic culture and evangelical fervour supplies the answer. Before the death of John Wesley, the Dissenting meeting-house was beginning to give way to the large Dissenting chapel. Surrey Chapel, on the south bank of the Thames, where Rowland Hill ministered from 1784 to 1833, is a typical example. Surrey Chapel seated two thousand people. It was the scene of the first extended organ recitals given in England, because it not only possessed an instrument (not to be thought of in a meeting-house), but had a better and more complete one than any Anglican church in London. The family has given place here to the massed congregation, and this technique of massed congregations appealed to Dissent in a manner which the Dissenters of the seventeenth century would have found incomprehensible. Preaching gradually developed, in the new large towns, out of the pattern of patient and formal exposition into the pattern of red-hot exhortation and dramatic religious demagogy. Robert Hall and later C. H. Spurgeon, Baptists, Joseph Parker and R. W. Dale, Congregationalists, James Martineau, Unitarian, and Hugh Price Hughes, Methodist, were the leaders each in his day of the 'large congregation' school of preaching. To accommodate the great congregations the meeting-houses were often pulled down to make way for large edifices 'in the Gothic style' (to quote from one existing minute-book of the time) that should accommodate four-figure congregations in crowded pews, and should be in their outward architecture eloquent of the ambition and success of Dissent. This was, as it were, an attempt to reproduce under cover of a roof the open-air evangelism of the Wesleys, and although in practice the great Dissenting chapels (Methodist-like, they were content to call them chapels) in the large cities were not in themselves so much centres of Evangelism as bases from which Evangelistic movements were sent to poorer districts, their intellectual and political influence was very considerable. The worst aspect of all this was the tendency to treat the preacher much in the same fashion as the film-actor is now treated, and to regard public worship as something like a respectable public entertainment. There was, with all the pomp and circumstance of the new-rich nonconformity, a softness at the centre which too often made the new Puritans content with cheap but pretentious buildings, second- and third-rate music, and a sentimentality in popular religion which a realistic twentieth-century generation has justifiably rejected. There was, too, a tendency for the mill-owner to go to one church and the mill-hand, if he went anywhere, to go to another. This, indeed, settled down into the habit of leaving the large Congregational church to the employer, and filling the Methodist missions with his employees. Nonconformity has in this present century paid dearly for its follies, and the unhappier aspects of Victorian nonconformity have been too widely celebrated both by historians and by anti-clerical novelists to need labouring here.

But the reasons for this huge success on nonconformity's part were the ancient connexion between Puritanism and the section of society which especially prospered under Victoria, together with the mass-techniques at which the Evangelical Revival had hinted. The Puritans of the nine-teenth century began to dream, and alongside their dreams of social reform and their dreams of massive success went less pleasant dreams which are better described as delusions of grandeur.

It was natural that the denominations at this time should begin to form themselves into connected and centralized bodies. The General Baptists (who by that title are distin-guished from 'Strict Baptists') formed a national union in 1813, and the Congregationalists did likewise in 1831.[9] Methodism had been a 'Connexion' since the foundation of Conference in 1784. It was all part of the new spirit of success. The unions were formed in order that a certain kind of efficiency, which again would have been a foreign notion to the classic Puritans, might inform the activities of the denominations. County groups, in each case, pre-ceded the national unions by about a generation. John Angell James, minister of Carr's Lane Chapel, Birmingham (a typical example of the 'large chapel' pattern) said in 1822 to his fellow Congregationalists that union was desirable for the purposes of more effective Evangelism: 'United fires', he said, 'brighten each other's blaze and increase each other's intensity; and thus the association of

churches enkindles each other's zeal, and provokes one
another to love and good works.' Union was also a good
defence against any renewed attempts at persecution or
local vexation that might appear. And it gave each local
church and member the feeling of 'belonging' to something large and safe.

5. *Worship*

One other aspect of Dissent is worth mentioning here,
and that is the beginning, at this same period, of radical
changes in its habits of worship which went along with the
new generalized techniques of church-going. The austere
simplicity of the meeting-house had to be modified for the
sake of a large and generalized congregation just as
naturally as the outward aspect of the church had to be
modified in order to attract them. What was tolerable when
everything was 'in the family' might well be a failure when
a large congregation consists of people who hardly know
one another. What 'in the family' is intimate and secure
might, in a general company, be boring or unintelligible.
Hence the new preaching-aesthetic. Hence the great
increase in hymn-singing. Hence the choirs with their
anthems and the large organs with their gifted organists
and romantic voluntaries. The new sense of distance
(romanticism again) which informed public worship—
symbolized by the placing of the pulpit now at one end of
a long building, not at one side of a square one—caused
certain Dissenting divines to utter a word which would
have been blasphemy in the ears of John Owen—'liturgy'.
Thomas Binney of the King's Weigh House Chapel,
London, addressed the Assembly of the Congregational
Union in 1843 on the subject of poetry, and wrote at
length on the desirability of decency and order in worship.[10]

Others wrote learnedly and persuasively on the question whether it was still necessary, or even right, for ministers to lead public prayer *ex tempore*. A somewhat hectic cult of beauty, disorganized and doomed to produce a sardonic reaction in later generations, overtook Dissent which, while it undoubtedly laid the foundations for much important thinking two or three generations later, issued at the time in embarrassing and monstrous aesthetic follies.

6. *Divisions*

But perhaps the real judgement on the 'success' of Dissent is to be seen in the terrifying fashion in which Dissenters tended to break away from each other during this same period. We have already mentioned certain splinter-groups that formed themselves in the Methodist following. We must now briefly refer to the sects of malcontents or enthusiasts that arose in the period of Dissent's greatest prestige. Many of these were malcontent Anglicans who, seeing the success of Dissent, decided to establish local Dissents of their own, and hoped later to be recognized as *bona fide* Dissenting bodies. The Plymouth Brethren, for example, have their origin in the secession of an Anglican priest, John Nelson Derby, who had held a living in Wicklow, but resigned in 1827 to form a body known as 'The Brethren', who repudiated all church order. Returning from Ireland to England he gathered many disciples, but schism developed within the movement with the consequence that one group at Plymouth (1845) and another at Bristol (1847) separated themselves from 'The Brethren'. The Plymouth group turned out to have the strongest survival value. An interesting curiosity in this group was that the only profession permitted to its members, who must otherwise either be Evangelists or labourers, was that of medicine. To this day the Plymouth Brethren have a high proportion of physicians in their ranks.[11]

The Catholic Apostolic, or Irvingite group, was founded by Edward Irving (1792-1834), a powerful but unbiddable Presbyterian preacher who was convicted by the General Assembly of the Presbyterian Church of heresy, and resigned to found his own group. A peculiar doctrine of the ministry, which required a special supernatural sign before new ministers could be ordained, led this group into ultimate difficulty, and at the present time it is being gradually absorbed into the Church of England.[12]

Of the sects of American origin that have enlivened the scene of English religion it is hardly necessary to speak here—Spiritualism, founded by Margaret and Kate Fox in New York in 1847, Christian Science (Mary Baker Eddy, 1875), Theosophy (Madame Blavatzky, New York, 1875), Seventh Day Adventism (William Miller, Pittsburgh, 1844), Jehovah's Witnesses (Charles Taze Russell, Pittsburgh, 1872), and the Church of the Latter Day Saints, or Mormonism (Joseph Smith, Utah, 1837). It is enough to say that none of these can by any stretch of imagination be called English institutions.[13]

It is, on the other hand, necessary to say a word about the Evangelistic episodes of the later part of the nineteenth century, especially the visits to this country of Dwight L. Moody and Ira D. Sankey. A distinguished American Evangelist, Dr Edwin Orr, has recently sought to show that in the year 1859 there was a marked revival of Evangelical religion in this country.[14] Whether this was a natural movement of Christians towards the increasing need to evangelize the industrialized masses, or whether at any point it was an organized movement, is somewhat in doubt. What is certain is that when Moody and Sankey first visited this country in 1867 they found an hospitable welcome for their evangelism, and they found waiting for them the undoubtedly indigenous organization of the Salvation Army (founded by William Booth in 1865). The Salvation Army was a direct attack on the ignorance and misery of the masses who were increasingly being lost to the Church. Moody and Sankey provided a spiritual rescue-squad designed to present religion to the lowest strata of society through simple preaching of two or three familiar doctrines and a folk-song equipment that virtually meant to the new proletariat what the carols had meant to the tougher medieval peasants. Moody and Sankey returned in 1872 for a three-year visit, and promoted what was not so much a revival of religion as a new religion among the dispossessed English peasantry. They and the Salvation Army helped each other. The Salvationists continued to seek out and help the destitute and forgotten people, and achieved and maintained the highest reputation for practical saintliness. Salvationism is, as it were, an unconscious or accidental Dissent, in as much as it does not at any point positively denounce any doctrine or discipline of the Church of England, but its organization is entirely self-contained, and it dispenses entirely with any sacramental practices. It is, therefore, to be reckoned among the Dissenting denominations—but for reasons far different from those which mark off the more historic Dissents. Moody and Sankey have been followed by a continuous line of American Evangelists; happily it is not necessary here to tell that story because it is no part of the story of English Dissent, although it is a very interesting, and somewhat unnerving, story of the development and the corruption of the methods of the pioneers.

For completeness, although historical sequence here breaks down, it will be well to mention four other significant Dissenting groups. The Connexion founded by Selina, Countess of Huntingdon, continues in separate existence as 'Lady Huntingdon's Connexion', although the greater number of its churches have been absorbed into Methodism or the Congregational Union. Lady Huntingdon, a disciple of John Wesley and of George Whitefield, gave herself up to religious work on the death of her husband in 1746, and sought to assist the Evangelical Revival by introducing the Evangelical faith to the upper classes. She supported Evangelical ministers, whether Methodist or Anglican, by constituting them her 'chaplains', but in 1779 the Church of England ruled that so far as their clergy was concerned, this was out of order. Accordingly she registered her chapels as Dissenting meeting-houses under the Toleration Act, and in 1790, the year before her death, she constituted her followers into a society. Though she quarrelled with Wesley, her aim was always to assist the work which he was leading; and even if Methodism as presented by her looked rather like a fashionable diversion for the leisured people at Bath and Brighton (where two of her largest chapels were built), her work was at least influential in attracting the attention of some of the few whom Wesley could not personally reach.

The Moravian Brethren, who form another small but not undistinguished body in present-day English Dissent, are an English version of the Hussite following, and can trace their ancestry back to Hus himself. As an English body they owe their foundation to Peter Bohler, who gathered a congregation in Fetter Lane, London, in 1738. This congregation the Countess of Huntingdon often attended, and John Wesley frequently preached to it in his early days: for it was (it will be recalled) from the German branch of the Moravians that he had derived so much of the inspiration that preceded his conversion. Moravianism still practises a form of cultivated pietism; it retains the offices of Bishop, Priest and Deacon; but its Dissent is primarily one of *ethos* rather than of discipline—an impatience with credal Christianity which in an earlier age would have placed them along with the Lollards but might not have driven them into that Dissent which by the eighteenth century had become a less serious and radical gesture than it was at the Reformation.

The Pentecostals, who have founded a large number of missions in Britain, are a sect of American origin, whose foundation dates back no farther than 1900; their greatest advance in this country came through the preaching of Stephen, George and Edward Jeffreys between 1925 and 1935. Divine healing and a certain religious enthusiasm characterize their belief and practice. The Pentecostals are also known as the 'Elim Foursquare Alliance' and their places of worship are frequently to be found in the larger cities of the country. At the time of writing (1959) their influence and publicity are increasing notably, and their earlier tendency to be obstinately schismatic has shown a marked decrease.

The Disciples of Christ, sometimes known as the 'Churches of Christ' and formerly as the Campbellites, owe their foundation to Alexander Campbell (1788–1866), who emigrated from Scotland, where he had a Presbyterian upbringing, to the United States, and there, becoming convinced of the rightness of adult baptism, gathered a congregation round him which was organized as a separate denomination in 1827. This body now has about a million members (in Britain, 15,000),

15 Mansfield College, Oxford

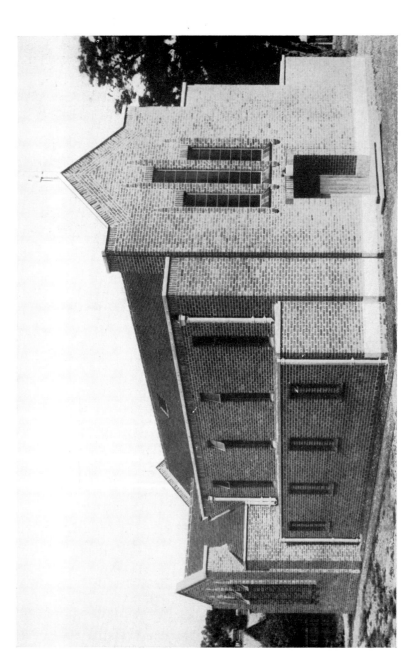

and is in effect a Baptist dissent from Presbyterianism. They follow orthodox Dissent in rejecting the use of credal formulae, but they have a high sacramental doctrine which enables them to celebrate the Holy Communion every Sunday (where Dissent as a whole remains content with a monthly or bi-monthly celebration). Their cultural *ethos* is more like that of educated American Presbyterianism than like that of those English Baptists with whom one might have expected them to seek union; but they have always been prominent in ecumenical work, and many universities in the United States owe their foundation to Disciples.

If this account of the varieties of nonconformity has given the reader some sense of the restlessness of English religion around the year 1900, it has done what was required. The picture is not even yet complete. Beyond these groups there is a large number of 'undenominational' places of worship, often advertising themselves simply as 'Free Church', not infrequently financed by one or two pious individualists, Conservative-Evangelical in theology and often perversely schismatic in behaviour. Romanticism was liable to encourage in men a sense of their own individual rights as well as, or instead of, a sense of their neighbour's, and the chief generalization which can be made about the nineteenth century in England, as about the fourteenth on the Continent, is that Christians fairly suddenly became uncommonly difficult to rebuke and impatient of criticism. A necessary accompaniment of this prevailing notion that if anybody criticizes you, or if you disagree with your co-religionists, you found your own church down the street is the collapse of any doctrine of discipline with the Church, and indeed the suspension of thought concerning the nature of the Church.

This is the underside both of Romanticism and of Evangelicalism, and the result of reaction against the inward-looking disciplines of classic Puritanism.

Notwithstanding the strange waywardness of nineteenth-century nonconformity in so many of its diverse activities, certain solid achievements in the direct line of the original intentions of Dissent can be recorded. Through the continuing activities of the Deputies, the rates levied on Dissenting places of worship were abolished in 1868, and the Burials Act, permitting the interment of Dissenters in parish graveyards, was passed in 1880.

7. *Education*

In the matter of education, once the principle of free education for all was established by the Education Act of 1871, the distinctive contribution of Dissent was (except for the organized rebellion against the education rate in 1902) confined to the theological field. Dissenters had already established several schools for the education of ministers' and missionaries' children, among them Silcoates, Taunton, Mill Hill, Bishop's Stortford and Eltham colleges; these have gradually been assimilated to the developing scheme of State education. But in the theological field the most notable gesture of Dissent was the founding of Mansfield College, Oxford, in 1886. All the denominations, of course, had by now their theological academies which by this time, for the reason just stated, had reverted to the strict theological curriculum of the early academies, but had become larger and properly staffed institutions. Mansfield, however, was a decisive gesture, since it was designed to provide in Oxford a Free Church theological faculty to balance the venerable community of Anglican professors who reside chiefly at

Christ Church. The project was Congregationalist in its inception; there had been since 1838 a college at Spring Hill, Birmingham, for the training of ministers for Congregational churches. The minister of Carr's Lane church, Birmingham, R. W. Dale, first suggested that the college be moved to Oxford, and that endowments be provided for its expansion. This was done, and in 1889 the buildings were opened. The records of that occasion show how impressive was the welcome given to the college by many of the Anglican academies of Oxford, and the subsequent record of the college shows that its founders' dream of of a Free Church faculty worthy to stand alongside the Anglican faculty have been abundantly fulfilled. Although the college was provided very largely by Congregationalist subscription, it has always been regarded as a place where any Free Churchman can be trained towards his ministry, and the eloquence of its external architecture bespeaks the intention of its founders that it should become more than merely a denominational training college. It received the status of a Permanent Private Hall in Oxford in the year 1955, and now accommodates undergraduates of all faculties as well as graduate theological students. Its staff has been drawn mostly from Congregationalism, but distinguished Presbyterians and (lately) American Lutherans have taught there.

Oxford now has Regent's Park College, moved there in 1827, for the training of Baptist ministers, which was granted the same status as Mansfield in 1957. Cambridge has three recognized theological colleges for Dissent: Cheshunt for Congregationalists, Wesley House for Methodists, and Westminster for Presbyterians.

In the matter of one other important item on the Deputies' agenda, that of Disestablishment, Dissent was less successful. Many moves were made to persuade Parliament of the wisdom of disestablishing the Church of England, and the opinion was often expressed from the Dissenting side that any alliance of ecclesiastical systems with civil power was unscriptural and unjust. In 1844 an Anti-State-Church Association came into being, which was in 1853 renamed the Liberation Society; this Society, though initially causing some embarrassment to the Dissenting Deputies—who as lawyers considered the new Society somewhat amateurish and incautious—worked closely with them; but their efforts came to nothing in England, although the more radically Dissenting temper of Wales brought about the Disestablishment of the Church in Wales in 1912. This issue is not at the moment a lively one in Dissent.

The Vicar of Bullhampton gives one picture of the ordinary Anglican's attitude to nineteenth-century Dissent: a graceless, strident, inconsiderate thing with neither manners nor sensibility. William Hazlitt, writing earlier, in 1819, set down a judgement of a different kind, with which this chapter may well close:

We are told that the different sects are hot-beds of sedition, because they are nurseries of public spirit, and independence, and sincerity of opinion in all other respects. They are so necessarily, and by the supposition. They are Dissenters from the Established Church; they submit voluntarily to certain privations; they incur a certain portion of obloquy and ill-will, for the sake of what they believe to be the truth; they are not time-servers on the face of the evidence, and that is sufficient to expose them to the instinctive hatred and ready ribaldry of those who think venality the first of virtues, and prostitution of principle the best sacrifice a man can make to the Graces or his Country. The Dissenter does not change his sentiments with the seasons; he does not suit his conscience to his convenience. This is enough to condemn him for a pestilent fellow. He will not give up his principles because they are unfashionable; therefore he is not to be trusted. He speaks his mind bluntly and honestly; therefore he is a secret disturber of the peace, a dark conspirator against the State. On the contrary, the different sects in this country are, or have been, the steadiest supporters of its liberties and laws; they are checks and barriers against the insidious or avowed encroachments of arbitrary power, as effectual and indispensable as any others in the Constitution: they are depositaries of a principle as sacred as and somewhat rarer than a devotion to Court-influence—we mean, the love of truth....Dissenters are the safest partisans and the steadiest friends.[15]

CHAPTER X

A NEW PICTURE

1. *The Ecumenical Movement*

The nineteenth century brought great changes to the fortunes of Dissent in England. They were as nothing compared with the changes in its *ethos* wrought by the events of the twentieth. The great difficulty before me in presenting this story at all has been, up to this point, constituted by the fact that all the Dissent about which I have written historically is something that is now strictly historic. There is nothing left, in the scene that the uncommitted observer sees in modern Britain, to correspond with the zeal of classical Dissent, the fervour of eighteenth-century Dissent, or the success of nineteenth-century Dissent. There is zeal here and fervour there and very notable success yonder, but they are of a different kind, attributable to different kinds of people, and their implications are different, from anything we observe in the historic ages before 1914. The reason is, of course, the ecumenical movement.

The ecumenical movement can be described historically by tracing the movements towards Church unity by dates and occasions over the last three-quarters of a century. For that kind of description the reader may be referred to the many excellent books that are now available.[1] Here I would be as brief about this as possible. What matters is to realize that the ecumenical movement has become a world-wide Dissent against denominational disunity, and that, operating as it does at every possible level, it represents the great Dissent of our time. The plane in which this

Dissent works is quite different from that of the historic Dissents, but the clamorous activity that accompanies it, and the distinguished and astonishing results it has achieved are of such magnitude and significance as to thrust almost all of the old categories of Dissent into the background of history.

Protests against disunity and inquiries into the justice of perpetuating historic differences have proceeded at all levels. Perhaps the most local and domestic form of the protest was to be seen in the movement in Independent Churches (of the Congregational or Baptist kind) towards local unions by counties, which began in the last quarter of the eighteenth century, and led naturally to the formation of national unions. Strict independency of the kind that was forced upon such bodies only by the rigours of persecution was seen to be a defective expression of the idea of the Church. From this equally naturally proceeded the movements towards Free Church unity that produced what is now known as the Free Church Federal Council.

A National Free Church Council was first formed in 1892, after a campaign lasting through some years, led by Hugh Price Hughes (Methodist) and John Clifford (Baptist). Its annual assembly was designed to deal with public issues, and to replace (although it did not force out of separate existence) the Dissenting Deputies. The social as well as the theological conscience of Dissent was to be expressed through it, and it was deeply involved in the protest of 1902 against the levying of rates on Dissenters for the support of Anglican church schools; a number of Dissenters went to prison rather than pay their rates or the fines for withholding rates. Their unity of purpose was expressed through the Free Church Council. In the election of 1906 the Council involved itself in politics, giving indispensable support to the Liberals.

This Council was an aggregate body rather than a gesture of corporate unity, and in 1919 J. H. Shakespeare, Secretary of the Baptist Union, caused to be formed a Federal Council of Evangelical Free Churches, which (unlike the earlier body) issued a statement of common faith (excluding the Unitarians), and was designed as a movement towards a united Free Church of England. These two bodies continued side by side until in 1940 they were merged in the Free Church Federal Council, which now acts as the forum for Free Church high-level debate and as the mouthpiece of Free Church policy *vis-à-vis* the other Christian bodies in Britain.

This protest of a limited kind against disunity implied a continuing Dissent against the Church of England. It also takes account of the fact that the Roman Catholic Church in England has once more become a significant and powerful religious body. Since the establishment of the hierarchy in 1850, which itself followed the removal of disabilities from Roman Catholics by the act of 1833, this Church has taken an increasing, though of course at most points a violently Dissenting, part in the religious life of the country.

But alongside this partial growth, there has been a radical change in the prevailing feeling between historic Dissent and the Church of England. This is a by-product of the wider work of the ecumenical movement, which has its origin in the nineteenth-century missionary expansion of the churches. The decisive date was 1910, when at the Edinburgh Missionary Conference, attended by representatives of missionary societies all over the world, the irrelevance of denominational differences on the mission-field was seen and clearly stated to be ground for inquiry concerning their relevance even in their originating countries. Commissions were set up under the names of 'Life and Work' and 'Faith and Order'. 'Life and Work' met at Stockholm in 1925, 'Faith and Order' at Lausanne in 1927; both met concurrently at Oxford and Edinburgh respectively in 1937, and it was there decided to merge the work of the two Commissions, and to implement the aims and prophecies of the Edinburgh conference of 1910, in the foundation of the World Council of Churches. The Second World War delayed this consummation until 1948, when on 22 August the first session of the World Council of Churches met at Amsterdam. The second plenary session met at Evanston, U.S.A., in 1954, and meetings of sub-commissions, with world-wide membership, have taken place in many of the world's leading cities since 1948. The World Council of Churches works primarily from Geneva, and is engaged partly in theological discussion with a view to the reconciliation of the churches of which it is com-posed, and partly in organizing a widespread and exceed-ingly well-applied programme of rescue work among the refugees of the world. The Roman Catholic Church plays no direct part in the World Council of Churches: that reconciliation is yet to be hoped for. But in the works of mercy which are conducted from Geneva, Roman Catholic bodies enjoy very close co-operation with the Protestants. In Britain the British Council of Churches is the World Council operating at the national level.

All this is enough to produce a radical change in the outlook of public-minded Protestant Dissenters, and in that of many of those whom they lead. Other influences which were brought to bear in the same direction at another level include the gesture of the Reverend Spencer Jones in

1900, who from an advanced Anglo-Catholic position proposed the setting aside of a day each year when Anglicans should pray for unity with Rome; this, after a good deal of correspondence and discussion, led to the observance of the week 18–25 January as a week of prayer for unity, under the blessing of Pope Pius X and the Anglo-Catholics in England. This was raised out of what might fairly be called a 'party' context by the gesture of the Abbé Paul Couturier who in 1932 began his annual series of 'calls to prayer'; Couturier, a priest of the archdiocese of Lyons, so convinced the Protestant world of the sincerity of his intentions that the observance of that period as a special 'unity week' has become widespread through the Anglican and Dissenting churches of many countries.

The ecumenical movement is appropriate, of course, to an age of speedy travel and swift communications. Its prophets could hardly have foreseen how well the natural development of technology would have served their aim. In our own country, the ecumenical movement has coincided with a marked regression of Dissent from its former position of prestige. This is unavoidable; and almost certainly, from the point of view of Dissent and of society in general, it is all to the good. Dissent cannot now stand for open hatred of Anglicanism, for Dissenters and Anglicans are meeting one another at all levels. At the universities students from all churches meet one another, and not infrequently marry one another. Inter-church conferences become increasingly popular. The Student Christian Movement and the Inter-Varsity Fellowship both tend to make young people at an impressionable age more conscious of the total mission of the Church than of the importance of their denominational peculiarities. Bishops and leading Free Churchmen know each other by their Christian names, and even if little success yet comes to conferences called with a view to promoting organic union between Dissent and the Church of England, much is achieved where such discussions can be carried on—as they are—in a climate where the real sorrow of schism has entirely replaced the rancour of the past. Dissenters and Anglicans attend each other's services without embarrassment (though not each other's Communion Tables). Books of weight and trenchancy are written from one side to interpret it to the other. Men are everywhere impatient of divisions which are as irrelevant and as embarrassing on the new housing estates of our cities as they are on the foreign mission field.

The spirit of William Temple—Britain's archetypal ecumenical figure—increasingly informs the episcopal bench; the Dissenters respond with utterances of such theological and spiritual breadth that their opposite numbers cheerfully accord them respect.[2] And while all the discussion goes on, the merciful work of the World Council of Churches continues under the joint leadership of distinguished men of many denominations, and the International Missionary Council continues to co-ordinate missionary work under a Congregationalist General Secretary.

In scholarship since 1900 the Dissenters have made so notable a contribution—this not least as a consequence of their being admitted to the older universities—that the Establishment has in this field also accorded them a deserved respect. Among Congregationalists, P. T. Forsyth, Alexander Souter, C. H. Dodd; among Methodists, Vincent Taylor, R. Newton Flew and Gordon Rupp; among Baptists, Wheeler Robinson, T. H. Robinson and H. H. Rowley, and among English

Presbyterians, W. A. L. Elmslie, H. H. Farmer and T. W. Manson—these write what every serious-minded English Christian must read; and this is to say nothing of the leaders of ecumenical thought, such as Nathaniel Micklem, Daniel Jenkins, Rupert Davies and Bishop (in South India) Lesslie Newbigin.

2. *The Limitations of Dissent*

This is all very well, but to the uncommitted reader it will begin to sound like unseemly trumpet-blowing. This is because, unless the reader is a Dissenter himself (in which case he will have found these pages markedly unsatisfactory) or an ecumenically minded Anglican (in which case he will already have read books to which this has nothing to add) the nature and doings of present-day Dissent will be quite strange to him. And the reason for that is that Dissenters have always been defective in those qualities which attract the attention of the ordinary man. We could have provided a much longer list of Dissenters distinguished in church matters than that which appears above. We could perhaps provide a respectable list of Dissenters who have gone into politics and remained faithful to Dissent. But Dissenting artists, novelists, poets, musicians (outside church)—where are they? The Church of England can claim as faithful communicants many who are of the highest distinction in those fields. Not so the Dissenters. Or to put it another way: the modern novel-reader will encounter many Anglican parsons in the stories he reads. Indeed, the era of the anti-clerical novelist is passing away, at least for the present, and many of the Anglican ministers he meets are intentionally agreeable characters. Roman Catholicism is abundant in its artists, and generous in its treatment of its own clergy in fiction.

But where in a novel or a good film will you find a Methodist or Baptist, Congregationalist or Presbyterian minister? They are not entirely absent, but they are far to seek.[3]

Dissent has traditionally attracted to itself people of the kind who are now stigmatized with the word 'bourgeois'. As Daniel Jenkins has shown,[4] it is the accountants and lawyers and shopkeepers who form the backbone of Dissent, rather than the artists, writers and men of leisure and substance. It is so rare as to become matter for jubilation in a nonconformist paper like the *Christian World* when somebody who catches public attention on a large scale—a successful author, an actor, a broadcaster, a television star—turns out to have had a Dissenting background and not to be ashamed of it. Titles are rare in Dissenting congregations—rarer than they were fifty years ago: service-men of high rank are not common; a few doctors and dentists, and a considerable number of schoolmasters and (even more) schoolmistresses, and a fair sprinkling of journalists. Local politicians were at one time very common in Dissent, but they have moved well away from it now. Men of the new scientific kind are increasing in Dissenting membership, but men of the older classical kind are decreasing.

Taking Dissent as he finds it, the ordinary intelligent man finds it on the whole uncommunicative about itself and incompetent in those larger social techniques which would 'put it over' or 'sell it' to him. He finds it most difficult to discover, without personal contact with one of them, what the Dissenters are saying, and therefore he finds it easy to be persuaded by those who say that Dissent still stands for those special policies that distinguished it in the time of his grandfather—pre-eminently, teetotalism and a jaundiced eye towards the theatre.

Dissent to him is philistine and morally worthy. 'Nonconformity' sounds to him slightly lifemanlike and uncomfortable. It lacks picturesqueness and public rhetoric.

Dissent can blame itself for a good deal of this. Traditionally its emphasis has been so much on the 'family' (which is one of the most dangerous words that have lately been coined as a synonym for 'the Church') as to make any who are not of the family very conscious of their being outsiders. It is not a family, but an institution, that advertises, and the Church has always been more of a family than an institution to Dissenters. If, for example, in the course of Dissenting worship some really wicked piece of music is badly performed, it has been the traditional Dissenting sentiment that 'such things hardly matter in a family'; it is as if auntie were asked to sing her song at a family party, and nobody would think of offering criticism, because everybody present loves auntie. Or if Dissenting public worship is carried on in a building that is aesthetically offensive, crowded with furniture, inwardly and outwardly not eloquent but simply garrulous—well, what does it matter? A man loves his home, never mind the architecture. Or if in the course of that worship, the congregation behaves in a manner that would strike the observer from outside as a curious mixture of the casual and the superstitious—chatting in conversational tones before and immediately after the service, remaining seated while the minister enters and while he speaks the opening words of the service, bawling the hymns and chattering during the collection, yet frowning profoundly on any child who presumes to fidget in his seat during the prayers or the sermon—why, all this is well enough provided you are 'the family'.

3. *Learning to be neighbourly*

The fact is that at this present time Dissent is learning how to live in the world with its neighbours. It is learning, in the age when the rhetoric has somewhat abated from its pulpit, the techniques of the rhetoric of behaviour. It is slowly learning how to communicate itself, and it is being embarrassed by those parts of its inheritance—buildings now admitted to be hideous, music now admitted to be repulsive, and even moral principles now admitted to be far from ultimate—which impede that communication. Dissenters now edit hymn books that take careful notice of what the Anglicans are doing; they are evolving a style of architecture that is designed not simply to be useful, and not at all to be portentous, but to express what they are saying inside the church; they are thinking about the liturgy of their churches, and they have all committed themselves to a radical overhaul of their sacramental thinking and habits.

True, Dissent sometimes takes the easy way of ecumenicity, and tries to behave as nearly Anglican-wise as possible, building churches with chancels and attempting cathedral settings of the Canticles. This is not of any significance, and it belongs to a generation just past.

It would be instructive to compare a typical successful Dissenting church of a hundred years ago with its counterpart today. The church in which the present writer was brought up was built in 1854 in a commanding position just off, but clearly visible from, the main street of a rapidly expanding town. The town combined a good deal of light industry, and one heavy industry (the railway) with a spectacular tourist trade. This church, seen from the main street, presents a south end with a large circular stained-glass window and beneath it a reasonably functional door. Its west side is built directly on to the street, and has a door and several windows of Gothic shape. Its east side is hard up against some rather seedy shop property, part of which it used to (and may still) own. Its north side is blank, being joined immediately to a large building containing rooms of various sizes for meetings and conferences and known as the 'Institute'. Underneath the church is a large and commodious hall seating perhaps 400 people. Already you have a sense of businesslike and not too untasteful worship: and (what you very rarely have in parish churches of this or earlier vintage) a clear indication that a great deal is expected to happen on church premises otherwise than in the sanctuary itself.

Within, the church seats something over a thousand people. It is packed with pews on the floor, and has a deep gallery round three sides. At the north end there is a central pulpit, in front of which is the Communion Table, and over which is an array of enormous organ pipes which becomes the natural focus of the observing eye wherever the observer may be sitting. (My own earliest recollections are of the pattern of those organ pipes.) The choir sit below the pulpit in six rows, three facing three, at right angles to the congregation, and the organist is behind the Table, between the two front choir-rows. Originally the choir sat in the back gallery and the organ was with them there (that is, at the south end, opposite the pulpit).

What does such a building *say*? It presupposes (and gets) a large congregation. It indicates that that congregation is there primarily to *listen*—hence the position of the pulpit. It indicates further that the preaching is what it comes to hear—hence the height of the pulpit. It indicates further yet that the congregation has pretensions to musical taste, which pretensions have somewhat softened the original austerity of the preaching-*ethos*—hence the fact that the pulpit stands a little lower now than it did before the organ pipes went in (this is deducible to a sensitive architectural eye). It is a lecture-hall with some attempt at a religious 'style'. But it symbolizes in itself nothing divine: there is no cross. Such stained glass as there is is decorative, not representative. As one Anglican friend said to me long ago (it was a lady of great devoutness), 'I should not feel uncomfortable in here without my hat'.

It is easy to contrast that pejoratively with the Anglican style. I here want, as a matter of social history, to contrast it with another Free Church style. Here, then, is a church in a residential suburb, built in the nineteen-fifties. The church is not now where the people work, but where they live and spend their leisure. It stands on a large plot of land which is not entirely covered by buildings. Some of the plot is used for ornamental gardening, some of it for a car park. The building is of domestic brick, and while it is not lofty, there is a sense of height in its general proportions. Over the porch there is a good-sized cross. The sanctuary forms one leg of an L-shaped plan, of which the other leg is used for what in the older church was called the 'Institute'. Within, the church is furnished perhaps with chairs, has a central aisle, and directs the eye to a central Communion Table behind which is a shallow apse with another large cross. The pulpit is on one side, on the other a lectern, and perhaps the console of an electronic organ. The church seats perhaps 300 people.

This building (it is a composite impression of any of several hundred post-war Free Church buildings) says something quite different from what the older building says. There is no demand here for a massive congregation. There is no mistaking the building for a lecture-room. It was obviously built when money was short and when prices were high; but, except in respect of the organ, which only too often is a harmonium left over from an older church and is rarely a very worthy instrument, the lack of funds is apparent in modesty rather than in cheapness of appointment. Above all, it is clear to any observer that this is a place for prayer and praise and for the celebration of the Sacraments as well as for preaching.

My friend would want to keep her hat on here. It 'looks like a church'. That puts it in a nutshell. Dissent of all denominations is now interested in what a church 'looks like' to the observer who is not a dyed-in-the-wool Dissenter. He is interested now in the impression he makes on the 'outsider'. He has taken the trouble to find out exactly what it is that he wants to say, and to find out how other churches 'say' more than his older churches did. He may fall into slavish imitation of traditions that do not go with his; he may be inept at discovering the essential principles of Dissent and contemporizing them. But that is what he has been busy doing for the last thirty years or so.

4. *What has Dissent to say?*

What then ought he to be saying to the world? What is his contribution to present-day culture and his place as an English institution? Clearly he is not now primarily occupied in vilifying and competing with the Church of England, although at any point he is entitled to protest against any remaining vestiges of snobbery and the Test Act mentality which may come to his notice (they still do here and there). But he is not now, or should not be, a man with a chip on his shoulder. Where, then, lies his Dissent?

It is quite fair to say that it lies where it always did lie, where, provided you are aware of the farthest history of Dissent, it can be seen to lie. If the Dissenter imagines that Dissent begins at 1662 he will go astray here. He will not understand himself, neither will anybody else understand him, if the material in the second and third chapters of this essay is ignored. Dissent in the form of grievance is now dead. But Dissent against obscurantism and spiritual tyranny is a force for which there was never so great need as there is today. For that, Dissenters have always stood.

They stood for it in the time of Wyclif; they stood for it at the Reformation; they stood for it in insisting on a good and accurate vernacular Bible; they stood for it in protesting against the tyranny of Charles I. They stood for it after the Restoration. They stood for it when the Harrow boys threw stones at the Baptist minister. They stood for it as Evangelicals protesting at the withholding of the faith from the poor, and as rationalists protesting at the spiritual disfranchisement of science; they stood for it as Bible critics who sought and found ways by which the primitive sense of the Scriptures might be disinterred from superstitious legends that had been imposed on them; they stood for it as Congregationalists who sought a New Testament form of authority in the Church, as Baptists who sought a rational interpretation of Baptism, as Methodists who sought an aristocracy of piety. But now every one of the things for which historic Dissent stood is not a grievance but a matter of controversy, and controversy, even when it is on so thorny a subject as episcopacy, is conducted with amity and reason.

Dissenters, until the day of total reunion of the Church dawns, will be wise to recognize in themselves several 'orders' in the Church Catholic. It is true and will remain true that in all Dissenting traditions there is a touch of partiality that robs them of true catholicity; it is chiefly to be seen in the fact that on the whole Dissent appeals to a certain class and kind of person, but not to all persons whatever. That there are different classes and kinds of person in the world, whom to reach requires different spiritual gifts, it would be foolish to deny. That in the present state of things Dissenters reach and minister to certain persons who without Dissent would find the Establishment unfriendly or inept may well be contended. But just as within the Roman Catholic Church prudence has insisted on the formation of preaching orders, contemplative orders, ascetic orders, pastoral orders, scholarly orders and other collocations of talent to meet the several needs of the total ministry of the Church, so, provided nobody gives way to complacency, we may regard Dissenters as entitled to develop and use those gifts which make each of their denominations a specially fit vehicle of the Gospel for certain large classes of people. Thus Daniel Jenkins argues for the special ministry of Congregationalism, boldly accepting the fact that Congregationalism is not in itself a truly Catholic body.[5] Thus also could any apologist of the other denominations argue. Taking the situation as we have it, and without pretence that the time has yet come for total reunion, this seems realistic.

5. *Alternative government*

But beyond this, we must surely wrestle with the notion with which this essay opened. I should here contend that we have not, in religious matters, reached the time yet when we can afford to dispense with Dissent as offering an 'alternative government', as a standing, though always charitable, criticism of that Establishment whose existence and logical priority Dissenters now accept. On the contrary, in an age of mass-movements, mass-enthusiasms, and mass-misdirections of opinion, a principle of Dissent is vital to a healthy society. In as much as the Church is a human society, this holds good of the Church.

Those who believe that all Dissent is religiously intolerable should read and ponder Joost A. M. Meerloo's book, *Mental Seduction and Menticide*—the most damaging indictment at present available of the conspiracy to induce, in secular affairs, conformity and self-betrayal in Western man.[6] Dr Meerloo is a psychologist of Dutch extraction, now resident in America, who has had experience both of undergoing 'brain-washing' and of healing those who have undergone it. His target is the tendency, often benevolent, to induce a breakdown of individuality, of personality, and of judgement in the mass-man by the agency of demagogy, advertisement, and (where relevant) totalitarian propaganda. He exposes what he calls the 'Strategy of Terror' through the murder of words, 'verbocracy and semantic fog', 'mental blackmail' and the deliberate manipulation of man's anxieties. He pleads eloquently for 'the nonconformist' (not, of course, in the religious sense), and for the working out of techniques that will enable men to resist demagogy and 'Big Brother' in whatever form he may be open to their attacks. In his peroration he writes thus:

The mystery of freedom is the existence of the great love of freedom! Those who have tasted it will not waver. Man revolts against unfair pressure.... Yet, when there is no will to prevent encroachments on the power of one by any of the others, the system of checks can degenerate. Like adolescents who try to hide behind the aprons of parental authority rather than face mature adulthood, the individual members of a democratic State may shrink from the mental activity it imposes. They long to take flight into a condition of thoughtless security. Often they would prefer the government, or some individual personification of the State, to solve their problems for them. It is this desire that makes totalitarians and conformists. Like an infant the conformist can sleep quietly and transfer all his worries to Father State.[7]

That, at any rate, we can all see happening: the power of the newspaper-owner, the power of the television-star, the power of the demagogue and the trades-union leader who deals in hatred and contempt. At the very time when the churches are looking and working for unity, unity becomes a thing of terror in politics. Men are unified by hatred and contempt more securely than they are unified by respect and love. To be one in moronic acceptance of a conformist party-line is a unity too seldom distinguished from that unity which the nations and the churches at their best are seeking.

It is hardly too much to claim that in the imperfect world in which we live the Church requires a principle of Dissent. Common experience tells us that, in its human aspect, the Church is liable to, and has indeed fallen victim to, most of the abuses that Meerloo ascribes to the politicians and technologists. Demagogy is far from unknown; mass-techniques inviting and encouraging supine conformity have lately become familiar.

It might be said, and with justice, that the whole Church should be a prophetic Dissent against all this. It is certainly true that the leaders of the Church in all its branches must occupy themselves more assiduously than they have been doing up to now with the implications of Meerloo, must protest against every invasion of human personality by culture or technology that tends towards the breakdown of the individual will to 'be a person' and thrusts men into blind and comfortable conformity. It is not true that

Dissent alone can do this, or should take to itself the special right to do it.

But this Dissent should do, and for this it still stands: it should propagate the notion of freedom and the right to criticize. It should still take the lead in suspecting any gesture, religious or cultural or political, that seems to be conformed to this special disorder of the world. It should dedicate itself to a leadership in mental religion, mental prayer, mental theology, to a crusade against the sentimentality which is but a stone's throw away from cruelty. And, leading thus in Dissent against what secular society accepts but what every church should reject, it should face the Establishment with constant criticism in matters of human government. During the Second World War the Opposition in Parliament agreed on certain fundamental principles with the Government, that it would not oppose. It would be a disaster if in peace-time any such agreement were made. In the Church it is rather different in as much as, in a sense, 'the war is on all the time'. Over a broad area, in 'unchristianized' Britain, there must be, and there have lately been found to be decisive matters on which there is no disagreement. The ecumenical movement has largely defined these. But at the level of human government, where the direction of church affairs must be undertaken by men who are dedicated to the Christian way but who are (as they all admit) defective in goodness and wisdom, it remains necessary for Dissent to be constantly, though it is necessarily a minority, in the position of offering 'an alternative Government'.

If it does that, and can emulate the politicians at least in their ability to divorce political opposition from personal hostility, Dissent can do its duty. Doing its duty is much more to the point than boasting of its history.

Discovering its duty is of more importance than reading an historical essay of this sort. But its duty will be better done if others understand it and wish it well, and if along with its own vain boastings we can clear out of the way the false rumours about it that inhibit the good neighbour's understanding of it. Dissent is an untidy, inconsistent affair. It is a very human affair. But nothing in its history is so staggering as this, that it has become an English Institution.

NOTES

CHAPTER I

1   Strathearn Gordon, *Our Parliament* (Hansard Society, 1945), p. 78.
2   'Ilico', *No More Apologies* (Hodder & Stoughton, 1940), p. 20.
3   Gordon, *op. cit.* p. 79.
4   Sir Charles Petrie, *The Jacobite Movement* (Eyre & Spottiswoode, 3rd ed. 1958), p. 23.

CHAPTER II

1   Sir Maurice Powicke, *The Reformation in England* (O.U.P. 1941), p. 1.
2   Gee and Hardy, *Documents Illustrative of English Church History* (Macmillan, 1896), pp. 145–467.
3   B. J. Kidd, *Documents of the Continental Reformation* (Oxford, 1911).
4   T. A. Lacey (ed.), *The King's Book* (S.P.C.K. 1932), p. xi.
5   Tertullian, *Adversus Judaeos*, 7.
6   Hugh Williams, *Christianity in Early Britain* (Oxford, 1912), p. 74.
7   *Ibid.* pp. 23, 28, 101–17.
8   William Langland, *Piers Plowman*, ed. Wells (Sheed & Ward, 1936), I, 109f.
9   G. Lechler, *John Wyclif and his English Precursors*, tr. Lorimer (1878), p. 466.

CHAPTER III

1   E. J. Hobsbawm, *Primitive Rebels* (Manchester University Press, 1959), p. 11.
2   R. A. Knox, *Enthusiasm* (Oxford, 1950), p. 75; H. J. Warner, *The Albigensian Heresy* (S.P.C.K. 1922), p. 62.
3   Hobsbawm, *op. cit.* p. 11; N. Cohn, *The Search for the Millennium* (1957).
4   George H. Williams, *Spiritual and Anabaptist Writers* (Library of Christian Classics, S.C.M. Press, 1958, vol. 25), p. 63.
5   *Ibid.* pp. 250ff.
6   *Ibid.* pp. 22f.
7   E. G. Rupp, *Studies in the English Protestant Tradition* (Cambridge, 1949), ch. 1.

CHAPTER IV

1 Jewel, *Apology for the Church of England* (1562, translated by Mrs Bacon, 1564), VI, 27.
2 R. Hooker, *Ecclesiastical Polity* (1597), III, 5.
3 P. Tillich, *The Protestant Era* (Nisbet, 1949), p. 210.

CHAPTER V

1 R. W. Dale, *History of English Congregationalism* (Hodder & Stoughton, 1884), p. 93.
2 *Ibid.*
3 W. H. Frere and N. Douglas, *Puritan Manifestos*, ed. Norman Sykes (S.P.C.K. 1954), pp. 8 ff.
4 *Ibid.* p. 29.
5 *Ibid.* p. 110.
6 *A True and Short Declaration...* (1582), f. A 3 verso.
7 C. Burrage, *The True Story of Robert Browne* (Oxford, 1906), p. 8; cf. F. J. Powicke, *Robert Browne* (Independent Press, 1910).
8 Robert Browne, *The Life and Manners...* (1582), § 44.
9 *Ibid.* § 51.
10 H. A. L. Fisher, *History of Europe* (one-volume edition, Arnold, 1936), p. 606.
11 W. Pierce, *A Historical Introduction to the Marprelate Tracts* (Constable, 1908), p. 148.
12 W. Pierce (ed.), *The Marprelate Tracts* (James Clarke, 1911).
13 Martin Marprelate, *Epistle*, in Pierce, *op. cit.* pp. 46 f.
14 Marprelate, *Mineralls*, *ibid.* pp. 185 f.
15 Marprelate, *Epistle*, *ibid.* pp. 60 ff.
16 D. Neal, *History of the Puritans* (1732), ed. J. Toulmin, 1837, I, pp. 332 ff.
17 *Ibid.* p. 333.
18 *Ibid.* p. 359.
19 *Ibid.* p. 336.
20 John Penry, *A Treatise...* (1590), B 1 verso.
21 Neal, *op. cit.* p. 336.
22 Barrow, *A Brief Discovery* (1590), ed. of 1707, pp. 275 ff. (This edition prints a text which differs at many important points from the original. The copy I have used, which is in the Library of Mansfield College, Oxford (5033 B 1), has been carefully annotated by R. W. Dale, who comments on the fly-leaf that the alterations are deliberate and tendencious.

Dale has in this copy restored the true text in copious marginal notes. The passage we here refer to contains no important divergences from the original.)

23 Barrow, *op. cit.* ch. XVI.

24 Neal, *op. cit.* p. 336. See also F. Higham, *Lancelot Andrewes* (S.C.M. Press, 1952), pp. 24f.

CHAPTER VI

1 Neal, *op. cit.* I, 369.

2 Calvin, *Institutes*, II, 16.

3 N. Sykes, in *The Bible To-day*, published for *The Times* (Eyre & Spottiswoode, 1955), pp. 140ff. See also many important *obiter dicta* in E. H. Robertson, *The New Translations of the Bible* (S.C.M. Press, 1959).

4 C. S. Lewis, *The Literary Impact of the Authorized Version* (University of London, Athlone Press, 1955).

5 C. Williams, *James I* (Barker, 1934; 2nd ed. 1951), p. 191.

6 C. Northcott (ed.), *Congregational Monthly* (May 1954).

7 J. Robinson, *A Just and Necessary Apology for Certain Christians no less contumeliously that commonly called Brownists or Barrowists* (1625).

8 See W. M. Hetherington, *History of the Westminster Assembly of Divines* (Edinburgh, 1878); A. F. Mitchell and J. Struthers (ed.), *Minutes of the Westminster Assembly* (1643–9, Edinburgh, 1874); S. W. Carruthers, *The Daily Work of the Westminster Assembly* (Philadelphia and London, Presbyterian Historical Societies, 1943); also S. W. Carruthers, *Four Centuries of the Westminster Confession* (Fredericton, N.B., 1957).

9 John Goodwin (*c.* 1594–1665), Vicar of St Stephen's, Coleman Street, London.

Philip Nye (*c.* 1598–1672), Vicar of Kimbolton, author of the Preface to the Westminster *Directory* of 1644.

Sidrach Simpson (*c.* 1600–55), Lecturer at St Margaret's, Fish Street, London.

Jeremiah Burroughes (1599–1646), Rector of Tivetshall, Norfolk, suspended 1633, lecturer at churches in Stepney and Cripplegate.

William Bridge (*c.* 1600–70), lecturer at Colchester and Norwich, later (1638) pastor of an Independent church at Rotterdam, returned to England 1642.

All these five were graduates of the University of Cambridge.

'Lecturer' here means broadly 'preacher', i.e. a minister without a 'living'.

10 S. W. Carruthers, *The Everyday Work* (see above), p. 47.

11 *Apologeticall Narration* (1643), p. 2.

12 *Ibid.* pp. 22–4.

13 *Some Observations and Annotations Upon the Apologeticall Narration* (1644).

14 John Owen, *The True Nature of a Gospel Church*, ch. IV (ed. John Huxtable, 1945), p. 51.

15 *Ibid.* ch. VII (ed. Huxtable), p. 85.

16 *Apologeticall Narration*, pp. 15–17.

17 See especially R. S. Paul, *The Lord Protector* (Lutterworth, 1955), and bibliography there provided.

18 H. A. L. Fisher, *op. cit.* p. 650.

19 R. S. Paul, *op. cit.* p. 218.

20 See Percy Scholes, *The Puritans and Music* (Oxford, 1936), and my own book, *The English Carol* (Jenkins, 1958), ch. VI.

21 Knox, *op. cit.* p. 142.

22 *Ibid.* pp. 163f.

23 C. Wilson, *The Outsider* (Gollancz, 1956), p. 216. The study of George Fox in this book, pp. 206–24, is of the greatest interest.

24 M. M. Knappen, *Two Puritan Diaries* (S.P.C.K. 1933), pp. 11–16.

25 G. R. Cragg, *Puritanism in the Age of the Great Persecution* (Cambridge University Press, 1957), p. 48.

26 H. Belloc, *How the Reformation Happened* (Cape, 1928; Life and Letters ed. 1933), p. 279.

27 Philip Doddridge, *The Rise and Progress of Religion in the Soul* (1740), XXI, 3–4.

CHAPTER VII

1 See Cragg, *op. cit.*

2 *The Savoy Declaration of Faith and Order*, newly edited by A. G. Matthews (Independent Press, 1958).

3 Baxter's Liturgy will be found appended to *Two Papers of Proposals Concerning the Discipline and Ceremonies of the Church of England* (1661). A bound collection of papers connected with these proceedings was published in London in 1661, and copies of it are still in circulation among theological booksellers.

An Accompt of all the Proceedings... in the above collection (1661).

4 See Horton Davies, *The Worship of the English Puritans* (Dacre Press, 1948), ch. VI. The most important research on these documents is embodied in a thesis by F. E. Ball, 'The Savoy Colloquy', deposited 1958 in the library of Mansfield College, Oxford.

5 Gee and Hardy, *Documents Illustrative of English Church History*, p. 601. Transcripts of all the Acts here referred to (except the first Conventicle Act) are to be found in that book.

6 Cragg, *op. cit.*

7 Cragg, *op. cit.* p. 97.

8 See especially R. Schlatter, *Richard Baxter and Puritan Politics* (Rutgers University Press, New Brunswick, N.J., 1957). Baxter's *Holy Commonwealth* (1659) contains some arguments which its author subsequently withdrew. In *The Life of Faith* (1670) he wrote of it, 'I hereby under my hand, as much as in me lyeth, reverse the book, and desire the world to take it as *non-Scriptum*'.

9 A. Grosart, *Annotated List of the Writings of R. Baxter* (privately printed, 1868).

10 *More Letters of Herbert Hensley Henson*, ed. E. F. Braley (S.P.C.K. 1954), letter 27, pp. 34 f. (written 1924 to the Rev. J. F. Lloyd Thomas).

11 G. M. Trevelyan, *English Social History* (Longmans, Green, 1944), pp. 263 f.

12 Fisher, *op. cit.* pp. 443, 677.

13 G. Burnet, *History of his Own Time* (Oxford, 1833), V, 434.

14 R. W. Dale, *History of Congregationalism* (1884), p. 505.

15 A. P. Davis, *Isaac Watts* (Independent Press, 1948), p. 59, quoting F. W. Wilson, *The Importance of the Reign of Queen Anne in English Church History* (Oxford, 1911), III, 514.

CHAPTER VIII

1 G. F. Nuttall, *Visible Saints* (Oxford, B. H. Blackwell, 1957).

2 Davis, *op. cit.* p. 23.

3 G. K. Chesterton, *George Bernard Shaw* (1914), p. 43.

4 I. Parker, *Dissenting Academies in England* (Cambridge University Press, 1914); J. W. Ashley Smith, *The Birth of Modern Education* (Independent Press, 1954).

5 Basil Willey, *The Eighteenth Century Background* (Chatto & Windus, 1950), pp. 17–20.

6 W. Jardine Grisbrooke, *Anglican Liturgies* (S.P.C.K. 1958), chs. IV and XIV.

7 E. Routley, *The Gift of Conversion*, pp. 23–8.
8 John Wesley, *Journal* (ed. Curnock, 1914), I, 475.
9 E. Routley, *The English Carol*, pp. 144 f.
10 E. A. Payne, *The Free Church Tradition in the Life of England* (S.C.M. 1944), p. 80.
11 B. L. Manning and Ormerod Greenwood, *The Protestant Dissenting Deputies* (Cambridge University Press, 1952). The facts in this section are extensively amplified in this source.

CHAPTER IX

1 C. S. Lewis, *De Descriptione Temporum* (Cambridge University Press, 1955).
2 W. Blake, caption with etching of Homer. *Collected Works* (Nonesuch edition), p. 583.
3 W. Blake, from caption to the Laocoon Group; *ibid.* p. 582.
4 W. Blake, *Jerusalem*, the closing words of Canto 52; *ibid.* p. 498.
5 C. S. Lewis, *The Pilgrim's Regress* (3rd ed., Geoffrey Bles, 1943), Preface.
6 R. G. Cowherd, *The Politics of English Dissent* (Epworth Press, 1959).
7 J. A. Patten, *These Remarkable Men* (Lutterworth Press, 1945).
8 N. Micklem, *The Idea of a Liberal Democracy* (Christopher Johnson, 1958) and *Aspects of Liberal Policy* (Liberal Publications, 1958).
9 For the history of the Baptist Union, see W. T. Whitley, *A History of British Baptists* (Carey Kingsgate Press, 1923); of the Congregational Union, A. Peel, *These Hundred Years* (Independent Press, 1932).
10 T. Binney, preface to the English edition (1856) of C. Baird, *A Chapter on Liturgies*.
11 W. B. Neatby, *A History of the Plymouth Brethren* (1901).
12 H. C. Whitley, *Blinded Eagle*, an account of the life and work of Henry Irving (S.C.M. 1955).
13 For brief accounts of the teaching of these sects, see Horton Davies, *Christian Deviations* (S.C.M. 1954).
14 E. Orr, *The Second Evangelical Awakening* (Marshall, Morgan & Scott, 1949).
15 W. Hazlitt, *Political Essays*, 1819 (Selected Works, ed. A. Ireland, London, 1889), pp. 88 f.

CHAPTER X

1   See Rouse and Neill, *The History of the Ecumenical Movement* (S.P.C.K. 1954); G. K. A. Bell (ed.), *Documents of Christian Unity*, series I–III (Oxford University Press, 1924–48); for Free Church movements towards unity, see E. K. H. Jordan, *Free Church Unity* (Lutterworth Press, 1956).

2   See, for example, D. T. Jenkins, *The Nature of Catholicity* (Faber, 1942), *Tradition and the Spirit* (Faber, 1951) and *Congregationalism* (Faber, 1954); Nathaniel Micklem, joint Chairman of the Lambeth Conversations, 1949–51, has done most of his ecumenical work in speech and personal encounter rather than in the literary field.

3   A notable exception to the generalization that nonconformity does not write or appear in fiction is Rachel Trickett's novel *The Return Home* (1948). These generalizations do not apply at all, of course, to Wales where what has always been Dissent in England has been a major factor in Welsh culture for the better part of three centuries.

4   D. T. Jenkins, *Congregationalism* (Faber, 1954).

5   Jenkins, *op. cit.* ch. IX.

6   J. A. M. Meerloo, *Mental Seduction and Menticide* (Cape, 1957).

7   Meerloo, *op. cit.* pp. 300f.

INDEX

Date Due Date Loaned			

Demco 38-295

I Am Glad

The Sound of GL

By Alice K. Flanagan

The Child's World®

I am glad the world
is a beautiful place.

3

I am glad glasses
help me to see it.

I am glad glue fixes
toys when they break.

I am glad my friend
keeps my secrets.

I am glad my sister has a gleam in her eye.

I am glad my Mom and Dad know how to cook.

I am glad light glows
in the dark.

I am glad I can go
to school.

I am glad I live
in a free country.

I am glad. Are you
glad, too?

Word List

glad

glasses

gleam

glows

glue

Note to Parents and Educators

Welcome to Wonder Books® Phonics Readers! These books are based on current research that supports the idea that our brains detect patterns rather than apply rules. This means that children learn to read more easily when they are taught the familiar spelling patterns found in English. As children progress in their reading, they can use these spelling patterns to figure out more complex words.

The Phonics Readers texts provide the opportunity to practice and apply knowledge of the sounds in natural language. The ten books on the long and short vowels introduce the sounds using familiar onsets and *rimes*, or spelling patterns, for reinforcement. The letter(s) before the vowel in a word are considered the onset. Changing the onset allows the consonant books in the series to maintain the practice and reinforcement of the rimes. The repeated use of a word or phrase reinforces the target sound.

As an example, the word "cat" might be used to present the short "a" sound, with the letter "c" being the onset and "–at" being the rime. This approach provides practice and reinforcement for the short "a" sound, since there are many familiar words with the "–at" rime.

The number on the spine of each book facilitates arranging the books in the order in which the sounds are learned. The books can also be arranged into groups of long vowels, short vowels, consonants, and blends. All the books in each grouping have their numbers printed in the same color on the spine. The books can be grouped and regrouped easily and quickly, depending on the teacher's needs.

The stories and accompanying photographs in this series are based on time-honored concepts in children's literature: Well-written, engaging texts and colorful, high-quality photographs combine to produce books that children want to read again and again.

Dr. Peg Ballard
Minnesota State University, Mankato, MN

About the Author

Alice K. Flanagan taught elementary school for ten years. Now she writes for children and teachers. She has been writing for more than twenty years. Some of her books include biographies, phonics books, holiday books, and information books about careers, animals, and weather. Alice K. Flanagan lives with her husband in Chicago, Illinois.

Published by The Child's World®
PO Box 326
Chanhassen, MN 55317-0326
800-599-READ
www.childsworld.com

Photo Credits
© Ariel Skelly/Corbis: Cover, 13
© Christopher Wilhelm/Corbis: 2
© Dann Tardiff/Corbis: 5
© Jerry Tobias/Corbis: 18
© Joe Bator/Corbis: 14
© Myrleen Ferguson Cate/PhotoEdit: 21
© Richard Hutchings/PhotoEdit: 17
© Romie Flanagan: 6
© Rolf Bruderer/Corbis: 9
© Royalty-Free/Corbis: 10

The Child's World®: Mary Berendes, Publishing Director
Editorial Directions, Inc.: E. Russell Primm, Editorial Director and Line Editor;
Alice K. Flanagan/Flanagan Publishing Services, Photo Researcher, Linda S. Koutris, Photo Selector

Copyright © 2004 by The Child's World®
All rights reserved. No part of this book may be
reproduced or utilized in any form or by any means
without written permission from the publisher.
Printed in the United States of America.

Library of Congress Cataloging-in-Publication Data
Flanagan, Alice K.
  I am glad : the sound of GL / by Alice K. Flanagan.
     p. cm. — (Wonder books)
Summary: Simple text features words that contain the consonant blend, "gl."
  ISBN 1-59296-157-6 (Library Bound : alk. paper)
  [1. English language—Phonetics. 2. Reading.] I. Title. II. Series:
Wonder books (Chanhassen, Minn.)
PZ7.F59824Iae 2004
[E]—dc22
                              2003018102

24